NO HIGHER POWER

NO HIGHER POWER

OBAMA'S WAR ON RELIGIOUS FREEDOM

PHYLLIS SCHLAFLY
AND GEORGE NEUMAYR

Since 1947
REGNERY
PUBLISHING, INC.
An Eagle Publishing Company • Washington, DC

Library of Congress Cataloging-in-Publication Data

Schlafly, Phyllis.
  No higher power / by Phyllis Schlafly and George Neumayr.
     p. cm.
  ISBN 978-1-62157-012-7
  1. Obama, Barack—Political and social views. 2. Obama,
Barack—Religion. 3. Religion and politics—United
States—History—21st century. 4. United States—Politics and
government—2009- I. Neumayr, George. II. Title.
  E908.3.S33 2012
  973.932092--dc23
                              2012022063

Published in the United States by
Regnery Publishing, Inc.
One Massachusetts Avenue NW
Washington, DC 20001
www.Regnery.com

Manufactured in the United States of America
10 9 8 7 6 5 4 3 2 1

Books are available in quantity for promotional or premium use. Write to Director of Special Sales, Regnery Publishing, Inc., One Massachusetts Avenue NW, Washington, DC 20001, for information on discounts and terms, or call (202) 216-0600.

Distributed to the trade by
Perseus Distribution
387 Park Avenue South
New York, NY 10016

CONTENTS

CHAPTER ONE

COERCED

O minous shadows fall beneath Barack Obama's "rainbow" of "hope and change." This book will illuminate the darkest one: his sweeping abuse of the American people's religious liberty— a right of conscience and free worship of God enshrined in the First Amendment of the U.S. Constitution.

The policies of the Obama administration represent the greatest government-directed assault on religious freedom in American history. In the 2008 campaign, candidate Obama promised a "transformative" presidency; as president, he has delivered one. Through stealth and sophistry, he is gradually transforming America into a secularist and socialist dystopia along modern Western European lines.

If you think his first term has been troubling, gird yourself for his second. "The future casts its shadow backwards," wrote the late British writer Malcolm Muggeridge. In January 2012, we saw a shadow of Obama's imagined future for America when he decreed, through his

Department of Health and Human Services secretary Kathleen Sebelius, that all employers, including most religious ones, pay for the contraceptives, sterilizations, and abortion-inducing pills of their employees.

"Today the department is announcing that the final rule on preventive health services will ensure that women with health insurance coverage will have access to the full range of the Institute of Medicine's recommended preventive services, including all FDA-approved forms of contraception," said Sebelius on January 20, 2012. "Women will not have to forego these services because of expensive co-pays or deductibles, or because an insurance plan doesn't include contraceptive services. This rule is consistent with the laws in a majority of states which already require contraception coverage in health plans, and includes the exemption in the interim final rule allowing certain religious organizations not to provide contraception coverage. Beginning August 1, 2012, most new and renewed health plans will be required to cover these services without cost sharing for women across the country."

Sebelius's phrase, "certain religious organizations," excluded the vast majority of religious schools, hospitals, and charitable institutions throughout the country. Obama had arrogated to himself the right to define which organizations qualify as "religious" and which do not. Most religious schools, hospitals, and charitable groups don't meet his definition, as it turns on narrow and unconstitutional criteria. Under Obama's definition, a religious institution must have "the inculcation of religious values as its purpose" and must "primarily" employ and serve "persons who share its religious tenets." That would obviously exclude Catholic hospitals, as well as many Catholic, Protestant, and Jewish schools and charities.

Regarding herself as generous, Sebelius informed horrified members of these groups that she was granting them extra time with which to adjust their religious views to the regulatory decree. "After evaluating comments, we have decided to add an additional element to the final rule," said Sebelius. "Nonprofit employers who, based on religious beliefs, do not currently provide contraceptive coverage in their insurance plan, will be provided an additional year, until August 1, 2013, to comply with the new law."

The secularist hubris of the Obama administration left religious leaders stunned.

"In effect, the president is saying we have a year to figure out how to violate our consciences," said a frustrated Cardinal Timothy Dolan of New York City.

The Union of Orthodox Jewish Congregations of America drew attention to Obama's outrageous presumption in determining for more than 300 million Americans that only private sects who exclusively serve their own are "religious organizations" worthy of conscience protection:

> Most troubling, is the Administration's underlying rationale for its decision, which appears to be a view that if a religious entity is not insular, but engaged with broader society, it loses its "religious" character and liberties. Many faiths firmly believe in being open to and engaged with broader society and fellow citizens of other faiths. The Administration's ruling makes the price of such an outward approach the violation of an organization's religious principles. This is deeply disappointing.

The announcement of Obama's fiat triggered a severe backlash of comments like these.

Obama had smugly assumed that birth control-using Catholics, Protestants, and Jews wouldn't care about the mandate. Bill Daley, his then chief of staff, warned him that he was walking into a political firestorm, according to Edward Klein, a recent biographer of Obama, in his book *The Amateur*. But the president ignored Daley's advice and instead listened to the likes of White House advisor Valerie Jarrett, a loud and influential feminist within the administration. Daley was proven right by the outcry that erupted after Sebelius's announcement, and a stung Obama had to cobble together a hasty "revision" to try to quell it in February 2012.

The "revision" amounted to nothing more than an accounting trick. Under it, insurance companies, instead of employers, are required to pick up the tab for contraceptives and abortifacients. "Religious liberty will be protected and a law that requires free preventative care will not discriminate against women," Obama implausibly asserted in the White House briefing room on February 10.

The heads of religious and conservative political groups, among others, scoffed at this statement. They denounced the change as an insulting distinction without a difference, noting that insurance companies would simply satisfy it by passing the costs of these "free" drugs to them in the form of higher premiums. Don't fall for this deception, said then-presidential candidate Newt Gingrich to Catholics, the group that generated the most intense criticism of the original HHS mandate. "I frankly don't care what deal he tries to cut; this is a man who is deeply committed. If he wins re-election, he will wage war on the Catholic Church the morning after he is re-elected," said Gingrich.

As we will detail in this book, Obama's HHS mandate marks just one of many battles in his unfolding war on religious liberty—a war that began with an opening shot in secularist San Francisco. Recall that in April 2008 candidate Obama—unaware that a blogger was recording his remarks at a private fundraiser for moneyed Bay Area radicals—dismissed religion as a consolation for the "bitter" in Middle America.

Contained within this one remark was the seed of secularist bigotry toward the religious that would come to full and odorous flower in his first term. Conservatives correctly noted that his "spread the wealth around" aside to Joe the Plumber on an Ohio campaign ropeline in 2008 foreshadowed his quasi-Marxist agenda of high taxation and confiscation of wealth. But less attention was paid by conservatives to his quasi-Marxist spin on religion.

Karl Marx famously belittled religion as an "opiate for the masses," a drug that the spread of worldwide socialism would one day make undesirable. Obama's aside in San Francisco about "bitter" Americans clinging to belief in God out of economic frustration was nothing more than a restatement of Marx's view of religion. Like Marx, Obama views traditional religion as a temporary opiate for the poor, confused, and jobless—a drug that will dissipate, he hopes, as the federal government assumes more God-like powers, and his new morality of abortion, subsidized contraception, and gay marriage gains adherents.

"You go into some of these small towns in Pennsylvania, and like a lot of small towns in the Midwest, the jobs have been gone now for 25 years and nothing's replaced them. And they fell through the Clinton administration, and the Bush administration, and each successive administration has said that somehow these communities are gonna regenerate and they have not," Obama said, warming to his theme in San Francisco. "So it's not surprising then that they get bitter, they cling to guns or religion or antipathy to people who aren't like them or anti-immigrant sentiment or anti-trade sentiment as a way to explain their frustrations."

Out of this Marxist mindset came the HHS mandate, his conveniently cramped definition of non-public "religious institutions," and his planned death of Judeo-Christianity by a thousand cuts.

But isn't Obama—skeptical readers of this book might ask—religious? Why would a president, who describes himself as a professing Christian, wage war on religious liberty? Isn't this charge just the usual partisan alarmism? No, it isn't. In this book we will demonstrate that Obama is a secularist ideologue first and a Christian second, if at all. (Even the Reverend Jeremiah Wright, Obama's pastor of many years, now doubts that he is a believing Christian.)

We acknowledge Obama's political skills and his apparent domestic virtue. By most accounts, he is a loyal husband to his wife and an attentive father to his children. But the evidence of his totalitarian secularist design on America's future is overwhelming. His toxic admixture of socialism and secularism—an ideology that he learned from his family, radical professors, his chosen pastor, and Saul Alinsky, among others—explains his habitual violations of the American people's God-given freedoms, and portends the even grimmer violations yet to come.

Obama calls himself a revolutionary—the "one we have been waiting for," as his starry-eyed supporters put it in 2008. But to what revolutionary tradition does he appeal? It is not the God-fearing American Revolution of our Founding Fathers. Rather, it is the starkly anti-religious tradition of the French Revolution. "Men will never be free until the last king is strangled with the entrails of the last priest," bellowed the Parisian intellectual Denis Diderot, whose thought contributed to the French Revolution. While Obama would never put his aims so crudely, his agenda points, albeit without violence, to the same end: purging the traditionally religious from public life.

In his beliefs if not his methods, Obama is a revolutionary of 1789 Paris, not of 1776 Philadelphia. "The audacity of hope," a phrase and concept that he adopted from Jeremiah Wright, the racist and socialist Chicago pastor who baptized his daughters and presided at his wedding, signifies a radical form of liberal Christianity without Christ that seeks to secularize everything, including religion itself.

We will show in this book that Obama is working to build not a glorious America under God, but one nation under coercive secularism. By reducing religion to the status of a wholly private sect, by silencing God's voice in public affairs, Obama seeks to monopolize civic life. In his imagined America, no higher power exists than godless government.

CHAPTER TWO

ONE NATION UNDER OBAMA

B arack Obama often casts himself as a "tolerant" liberal. He prides himself on having grown up in the carefree, Aloha-style atmosphere of Hawaii, a place of "aborted treaties and crippling diseases brought by the missionaries" (as he put it in his first memoir, *Dreams from My Father*) that he grew to love. He has also highlighted his years spent in the ethnic diversity of largely Islamic Indonesia. The Islamic call to prayer is the "most beautiful sound in the world," he once said while musing upon his childhood spell in Jakarta.

He has written about attending college in casual, diverse California and in the melting pot of New York City, attending law school with the best and brightest at Harvard, and then settling into Chicago, where he became a community organizer on the city's downtrodden South Side. Throughout his life he has thought of himself as a "progressive," pushing for more expansive rights, justice, and opportunity for the oppressed.

But his much-advertised tolerance contains a bald contradiction: it permits him to behave intolerantly towards conservative Americans, particularly religious ones. His record on the issue of religious freedom is one of blatant intolerance. It reveals a consistent prejudice in favor of a secularist federal government that has no qualms about bullying the religious, even to the point of dictating which ministers their churches can hire and fire.

Exhibit A of this secularist arrogance is the October 2011 Supreme Court case of *Hosanna-Tabor Evangelical Lutheran Church and School* v. *EEOC*. Before the high court, Obama's lawyer for the Equal Employment Opportunity Commission made the astonishing argument that the federal government could force a Lutheran church to rehire a teacher/minister for its school, after religious officials there had decided to hire someone else and after the rejected teacher/minister had violated church procedures.

The school, affiliated with the Missouri Synod of the Lutheran Church, had conferred on the teacher the title of "Minister of Religion." The school fired her after she violated the rules of the church by threatening to sue it under the Americans with Disabilities Act. The teacher/minister then filed a complaint with the EEOC, which in turn successfully sued the school and demanded that it hire her back.

The case ended up in the U.S. Court of Appeals for the Sixth Circuit, which ruled against the church school. In 2011, the Supreme Court took the case up and concluded that the EEOC had openly defied what federal courts have long recognized: a "ministerial exception" to federal employment laws—the exception covering, among others, priests, rabbis, and Protestant ministers subject to religious authority.

Even Obama's former solicitor general and now a Supreme Court Justice, Elena Kagan, couldn't believe her ears when the EEOC's lawyer, Leondra Kruger, claimed that the Evangelical Lutheran Church's ministerial hiring and firing decisions enjoyed no First Amendment protections:

JUSTICE KAGAN: Do you believe, Ms. Kruger, that a church has a right that is grounded in the Free Exercise Clause and/or the Establishment Clause to institutional autonomy with respect to its employees?

MS. KRUGER: We do not see that line of church autonomy principles in the Religion Clause jurisprudence as such. We see it as a question of freedom of association. We think that this case is perhaps one of the cases—

JUSTICE KAGAN: So, this is to go back to Justice Scalia's question, because I too find that amazing, that you think that the Free—neither the Free Exercise Clause nor the Establishment Clause has anything to say about a church's relationship with its own employees.

Kagan was referring to the colorful moment earlier in the hearing when Kruger had told Justice Antonin Scalia that religious organizations and secular businesses should be seen as exactly the same under the Constitution. Scalia had exploded at this remark: "That's extraordinary! There, black on white in the text of the Constitution, are special protections for religion. And you say it makes no difference?"

The Obama administration's case was so flimsy and ludicrous that it ended up losing 9 to 0 in January 2012.

This unanimous rebuke from the Supreme Court would have given most presidents pause. Not Obama. In the very next month, he pulled the trigger on his Health and Human Services order coercing most religious employers into paying for the contraception and abortion-inducing pills of their employees. Within two months Obama had discovered two new rights: Americans could not only demand a job from their church but also demand that that church pay for their sex lives.

The Obama administration regards contraceptives and abortifacients as essential services to be provided free of charge by "public" religions for the sake of "women's health." How aborting embryos and rendering functioning parts of the body sterile meet any normal definition of "health" has never been explained by Kathleen Sebelius. Obama's commissars within the bowels of the HHS have declared it "health," she says, and that's that.

Called to testify before Congress, Sebelius had no coherent answers to offer outraged conservatives. Pennsylvania Congressman Tim Murphy asked her, "Who pays for it? There's no such thing as a free service." Sebelius replied: "The reduction in the number of pregnancies compensates for cost of contraception."

"So you are saying, by not having babies born, we are going to save money on health care?" asked an astonished Murphy.

In Obama's America, pregnancy is a curse (he once said, on the campaign trail in 2008, that if his daughters made "a mistake" he didn't want them "punished with a baby"), fertility is a disease, and contraception and death represent a final solution to deficits.

In 2009, Nancy Pelosi made a crass comment not unlike Sebelius's on the economic efficiency of not having children, as she explained Obama's reasons for including millions of dollars in new spending for contraceptives and abortifacients in his "Stimulus package." "It will reduce costs," a coldly utilitarian Pelosi claimed. France and Russia, among other demographically challenged countries, pay parents to have children; Obama pays parents to "stimulate" the economy by killing theirs. Jonathan Swift's literary work *A Modest Proposal* has gone from satire to stimulus.

When asked by another congressman about the constitutionality of the HHS mandate, Sebelius revealed that she hadn't even bothered to study the matter. "So, before this rule was promulgated," Congressman Trey Gowdy asked, "did you read any of the Supreme Court cases on religious liberty?"

"I did not," Sebelius answered. Gowdy asked her about a series of cases in which the Supreme Court sided with religious groups. Sebelius said that she wasn't aware of those cases or the reasoning that went into them. "I'm not a lawyer, and I don't pretend to understand the nuances of the constitutional balancing tests," Sebelius told him, causing titters of muffled laughter in the room.

MINDLESS PROPAGANDA

All the HHS secretary knows is what "experts" tell her: that contraception and abortion are indispensable supports to the "well-being" of women. Under this mindless propaganda, not only can the federal government require insurers to provide them and employers to offer them, but this new "right" to free contraception and abortifacients trumps the right of conscience covered by the First Amendment's guarantee of the free exercise of religion.

To Obama, religion has no freedom outside of a church and sometimes not even there, judging by his administration's EEOC policy. Previous presidents have peppered their speeches with references to "religious freedom." Obama prefers the narrower phrase, "freedom of worship." (Journalists have studied his speeches and found that phrase in them far more often than "religious freedom.") This rhetorical shift is freighted with meaning, as it implies that Obama considers religion a purely private matter. Cardinal Francis George of Chicago, among others, has drawn attention to the president's sleight of hand here:

> Liberty of religion is more than freedom of worship. Freedom
> of worship was guaranteed in the Constitution of the former
> Soviet Union. You could go to church, if you could find one.
> The church, however, could do nothing except conduct religious
> rites in places of worship—no schools, religious publications,

health care institutions, organized charity, ministry for justice, and the works of mercy that flow naturally from a living faith. All of these were co-opted by the government. We fought a long, cold war to defeat that vision of society.

The strangest accusation in this manipulated public discussion has the bishops not respecting the separation between church and state. The bishops would love to have the separation between church and state we thought we enjoyed just a few months ago, when we were free to run Catholic institutions in conformity with the demands of the Catholic faith, when the government couldn't tell us which of our ministries are Catholic and which not, when the law protected rather than crushed conscience. The state is making itself into a church. The bishops didn't begin this dismaying conflict nor choose its timing.

Several Catholic prelates, including Cardinal George, have warned that unless the HHS mandate is rescinded, Catholic hospitals—which form one of the largest private providers of health care in the country—will go out of business in 2014. The price tag for refusing to comply with Obamacare's fiat is $2,000 per employee. This bill of fines will add up quickly for Catholic hospitals that employ thousands and that provide millions of dollars worth of free and charitable care to the indigent. The fines will effectively bankrupt these hospitals.

Catholic hospital directories may soon become "souvenirs," wrote Cardinal George near the beginning of Lent in 2012:

What will happen if the HHS regulations are not rescinded? A Catholic institution, so far as I can see right now, will have one of four choices: 1) secularize itself, breaking its connection to the church, her moral and social teachings and the oversight of its ministry by the local bishop. This is a form of theft. It means the church will not be permitted to have an institutional voice in public life. 2) Pay exorbitant annual fines to avoid paying for insurance policies that cover abortifacient drugs, artificial contraception and sterilization. This is not economically sustainable. 3) Sell the institution to a non-Catholic group or to a local government. 4) Close down....

If you haven't already purchased the Archdiocesan Directory for 2012, I would suggest you get one as a souvenir. On page L-3, there is a complete list of Catholic hospitals and health care institutions in Cook and Lake counties. Each entry represents much sacrifice on the part of medical personnel, administrators and religious sponsors. Each name signifies the love of Christ to people of all classes and races and religions. Two Lents from now, unless something changes, that page will be blank.

The cardinal's apocalyptic tone is justified. His realistic scenario of shuttered Catholic hospitals would make most administrations hesitate. Not this one. The Obama administration remains blithely indifferent to that prospect. The administration takes the view that contraception and abortifacients are morally good, and that the state is perfectly justified in mandating such moral goods. Private institutions, like churches, aren't granted, under Obama's view, any real independence. They are vehicles for the state and for the Obama administration in particular to enact social change and policies of which it approves. By standing in the way of progressive "social reform," according to this view, the Catholic Church forfeits her freedom and deserves to be co-opted or shut down.

Cardinal Timothy Dolan of New York City revealed in a March 2012 letter that Obama's aides had sought to lecture him and other bishops on what Catholicism *should* mean. The aides used an editorial written by political liberals at the Jesuit magazine *America* as part of their lecture. Dolan wrote:

> At a recent meeting between staff of the bishops' conference and the White House staff, our staff members asked directly whether the broader concerns of religious freedom—that is, revisiting the straight-jacketing mandates, or broadening the maligned exemption—are all off the table. They were informed that they are. So much for "working out the wrinkles." Instead, they advised the bishops' conference that we should listen to the "enlightened" voices of accommodation, such as the recent, hardly surprising yet terribly unfortunate editorial in *America*. The White House seems to think we bishops simply do not know or understand Catholic teaching and so, taking a cue from its own definition of religious freedom, now has nominated its own handpicked official Catholic teachers.

The German sociologist Max Weber coined the term "caesaropapism," defining it as "the complete subordination of priests to secular power." Were Weber alive today and living in America, he might have revised the term and called it Obamaopapism.

Is this what the American people want? A president who treats the U.S. bishops in a manner similar to Joseph Stalin's control of the Orthodox clergy? Stalin turned cowed Orthodox bishops and priests into stooges for state propaganda and fiats; Obama endeavors to do the same with threatened monks, nuns, priests, pastors, and rabbis. He expects them, if they wish to enter the public square, to bless his secularism or shut up.

The Obama administration has tried to paint Republicans who defend the Catholic Church's autonomy as combatants in a "war on women." You see, the liberation theology Obama learned at the knee of the Reverend Wright—and the entire leftist narrative of "brave liberals" fighting for aggrieved groups—aims at lifting political oppression. Anyone who opposes the Obama administration, or the march of leftist progress, must ipso facto be an oppressor. The fact remains, however, that Obama is the one waging war—he is attacking the freedom of men and women of religious faith to abide by their beliefs. Obama is the cocky victimizer who likes to play the victim.

Most Americans have never regarded the absence of federally mandated contraception and abortifacient coverage in health insurance as a form of oppression; and the real effect of the law is a much more radical one: establishing the federal government as the arbiter of acceptable religious teaching and practice in public life—and not for some obscure sect with outlandish beliefs, but for the largest Christian denomination in the United States and in the world.

Most Americans do not yet grasp the depth of Obama's contempt for religious freedom. His secularist view of it floats above the Constitution—which he once dismissed in a radio interview as flawed and stunted—and America's long history of religious freedom. If the "separation of church and state" means anything—and it is well to remember that this unhelpfully vague phrase comes not from the Constitution but from a letter by Thomas Jefferson, who was not at the Constitutional Convention (he was serving as ambassador to France at the time)—it means the separation of the federal government from religious activity at the state and local level.

The Founding Fathers did not want the federal government to impose a national religion. They feared replicating in America an institution like the Church of England, which would set at the federal level an official religious denomination for the United States. They wanted not only to protect individual conscience, but also to protect the religious freedom of the states. Six states, in fact, refused to accept the U.S. Constitution until it was made clear that the First Amendment prevented the federal government from imposing a national church on them. Here is an important and neglected fact: those six states that finally signed the Constitution *ran established churches.*

It is indisputable that the First Amendment was written *not* to suppress those state churches but to protect them from the federal government. Leaders from those six states would have never signed the Constitution otherwise. They insisted on the language, "Congress shall make no law respecting an establishment of religion, or prohibiting the free exercise thereof," to make clear that the federal government had no right to establish its own religion and *disestablish* theirs. In other words, the supposed "wall of separation" contained in the Constitution is not between government and religion but between the federal government and the peoples' religious activities within individual states.

The Founding Fathers' fear of a federally mandated religious orthodoxy has not been achieved by any recognizable Christian denomination. But it has been achieved by an Obama administration that is intent on imposing a federal religion of secularism on the states and on the people.

If you don't want to underwrite the contraceptive-driven promiscuity of your employees, well, too bad, says Obama in effect. He has created a "right" to contraception that trumps your right to conscience. In Obama's politicized mind, it is more important to wow secularists and leftist feminists than to honor the Founding Fathers and the Constitution they framed. Just as the Constitution was "flawed" by its initial failure to recognize the civil rights of black Americans, according to his logic, so too is it flawed in myriad other ways, including its failure to recognize a constitutional right to subsidized condoms, IUDs, and contraceptive pills.

The notion that American citizens enjoy a constitutional right to force employers to underwrite their sex lives would have left George Washington and the other Founding Fathers baffled and near speechless. Where,

Washington might have asked a brazen colonial barmaid taken with that notion, does such a right originate? Does it come from God? Surely not; it can only come from the whims of a degraded regime of fallen and deluded men. Who else would dare dignify such an absurdity as an "inalienable right"?

The Constitution's Framers always assumed that the American people's basic Christian assumptions, regardless of denominational differences, had a rightful role in guiding law: the Founders did not assume that they needed to draw up a new standard of morality, a new ten commandments, a new golden rule. They assumed that their rights were God-given rights. But the Obama administration, with much leftist precedent behind it, has overturned this assumption. Not only does Christianity have no rightful role in guiding law, under Obama's secularist philosophy, but it is the federal government that stands as the arbiter of moral standards and justice, and can overturn whenever it wants traditional Judeo-Christian principles, whether the issue is subsidized contraception or a ban on open homosexuals in the military.

IN THE FEDERAL GOVERNMENT WE TRUST

America's currency still says, "In God We Trust." But under the Obama administration it might as well say, "In the Federal Government We Trust." Under Obama, government, not God, holds itself out as the sole measure of morality and rights; government, not God, is the determiner of the "common good." Never mind that the word "good" derives from the word God; in practical terms, to the Obama administration, the word "good" derives from the word government.

The actions of the Obama administration represent a final phase in the unfolding of modern liberalism's radical and implicitly atheistic ideology, an ideology which is tantamount to a man-centered willfulness writ large. Under this arrogance the caprice of central planners replaces traditional Judeo-Christian, not to mention constitutional, restraints on power. The fluctuating and often corrupt desires of arrogant men form the measure of "good government." As the grim chapters of recent history show—from the 100 million people put to death under atheistic communism, to the 25 million executed by the pagan National Socialists, to the millions of unborn children whose lives have been sacrificed on the altar of modern convenience—taking God out of "goodness" (the Communists, the National Socialists, and the abortionists all believed that they were doing "good") drains the term of any coherent meaning, leaving humans at the mercy of power-seeking ideologues.

On one level, Obama appears like a harmless, if glib and empty, pol, who careens from focus group to pollster as he stumbles towards a second term. But on another level, buried deep within his curious and amorphous personality, he is a man of perverse tenacity, a convinced socialist and secularist who was trained long ago to run the ball into the end zone for radicalism.

For all his joshing and superficial charm, he remains, ideologically, a committed and even mean leftist—part Diderot, part Alinsky—a secular demigod, at once smiling and pitiless, presented to an unredeemed people amidst the backdrop of oversized and plastic Greek columns at the Democratic National Convention in 2008.

Such a hyped and messianic Democratic president was bound to overreach disastrously. Obamacare is a "big f---ing deal," acolyte Joe Biden whispered into the chosen one's ear. And it is—an unconstitutional "big f---ing deal" disguised as altruistic legislation that was rammed through Congress by blind and reckless partisans who hadn't even read it.

But the leftist central planners in the bureaucracy and the social engineers from Planned Parenthood had reviewed the bill carefully. The triumph of the legislation in the House of Representatives, on the eve of Christmas no less, left them dizzy with excitement, as they knew its

unread provisions would soon become nooses for the religious conservatives they hate.

"Darn tooting," Obama declared to his most militant and fervent
supporters—abortion-rights feminists who demanded to know from
him during a campaign stop in fall 2011 if he was going to make good on
his promise to manhandle the Catholic Church over contraception and
abortifacients.

Make no mistake about the brutal logic of the Obama administration's conception of rights, as in the right to "free" contraception: not
only must everyone submit to the administration's mandated rights, but
the government then assigns to itself the task of punishing those who
resist. Who, for example, cares if Christian schools object to financing
the fornication of their students? Those schools are wrong, and error has
no rights, Obama implicitly argues.

Even if the Supreme Court overturns Obamacare, this contretemps
over its intrusive mandates marks a historic and illuminating moment
in the culture war. It is a crystallizing flashpoint in which the totalitarian-
ism and anti-religious bigotry long implicit in secularism finally rise to
the surface and become explicit for all to see.

Of course, flustered Obama aides, worried about the religious vote,
point to the narrow exemption in Obamacare for the Amish and other
wholly sectarian groups, and insist that this administration "respects
religious freedom." But it turns out that the Democrats didn't even want
to grant that insultingly narrow exemption. Illinois Congresswoman Jan
Schakowsky let this cat out of the bag in February 2012, as the *Hill* newspaper reported: "There's no need for the White House to adopt a wider
religious exemption. Carving out churches and other strictly religious
employers 'was in itself a compromise,' she said, noting that eight states
have contraception mandates without religious exemptions."

For all of Obama's reassurances about religion as a sacred "private"
matter, for all of his chic chatter about the "privacy of the bedroom,"

nothing in the end is actually private under the secularist regime of modern liberalism that he favors. No one is truly free to leave Obama's animal farm.

From the beginning of life to the end of life, from "free" contraceptives to rationing panels for the elderly, the big brothers and sisters of Obamacare are watching. And to sweeten their triumphant secularism even more, they will leave its steep and bloodied bill to their reviled religious opponents for final payment.

CHAPTER THREE

THE INDEX OF OBAMA'S HOSTILITY TO RELIGION

Barack Obama has compiled a record of hostility to religion that is unmatched by any other president in American history. Author David Barton calls Obama "America's most Biblically-hostile U.S. president." As commander in chief of the United States military, the office in which he enjoys unquestioned authority, he has been particularly aggressive in curbing religious expression. The military employs a high concentration of people who believe in God and Country—a formulation that Obama wants to replace with an allegiance to the State and its Progressive Social Engineering.

To give readers an idea of the scope of Obama's assault on religious freedom, here is a list, presented chronologically, that illustrates the ubiquity of his campaign to assert the power of the coercive secular state. (Some of the examples from the following list were first collected by Mr. Barton at his website, www.wallbuilders.com.) Where Obama sees Judeo-Christian principles and practice in public life, his goal is to erase, punish, or reverse them. Here is how he does it.

• One of Obama's first executive orders in January 2009 reversed the practice of the Bush administration and gave taxpayer dollars to non-governmental organizations that perform abortions abroad. It was a shot across the bow of traditionally religious Americans and an early assertion by the Obama administration that abortion is not only a publicly subsidized right, but even a taxpayer-financed universal right extending beyond our borders.

• In February 2009, Obama announced his intention to eliminate conscience protections that were designed to allow pro-life nurses and doctors who work at federally funded hospitals to opt out of performing abortions or other practices they consider immoral. President George W. Bush had established those protections in his final month of office.

R. Albert Mohler Jr., president of the Southern Baptist Theological Seminary, blasted the administration's announcement. "Gone are all protections for those who object by conscience to abortifacient drugs and 'emergency' contraceptives, the treatment of gay men and lesbians, and prescriptions for birth control sought by single women," he wrote. "In these cases, medical personnel have objected that their conscience and understanding of medical ethics do not allow them to facilitate acts and behaviors that are both immoral and unhealthy."

Mohler warned that "the Obama administration is now ready to use the coercive power of the state to force medical personnel to perform acts they consider to be morally wrong and unhealthy for their patients." He called it "a tyrannical trampling of individual conscience by the power of the state."

The Christian Medical Association, an organization that represents evangelical medical personnel, also decried the administration's reversal of Bush's protections and predicted that Obama's move would drive people of faith out of the medical profession and thereby hurt the poor, given that religiously motivated doctors and nurses provide much of their care.

The Christian Medical Association sent a letter to Sebelius—a letter also signed by the Catholic Medical Association and the American Association of Pro-Life Obstetricians and Gynecologists, among other groups—that warned of this exodus. The letter read in part:

> Without the protection of the full conscience clause outlined by the Bush Administration, healthcare access for hundreds of thousands of patients nationwide will be threatened and healthcare costs will rise because of the lack of facilities to provide needed services.
>
> Each year, one in six patients is cared for in a Catholic hospital. It is well known that these hospitals will not perform abortions. Without conscience protections, these institutions, which provide services to millions of patients, may shut down rather than be forced to perform surgical or medical abortions.
>
> While the Department of Health and Human Services did not rescind the conscience protections for abortions, the Department did rescind the protection for medical professionals in prescribing and dispensing proven abortion-causing drugs such as *ella* and Plan B and in performing in vitro fertilization, among other dangerous women's health procedures.
>
> Driving faith-based and conscience minded professionals out of medicine would strand hundreds of thousands of patients, especially those in rural vicinities who rely on only a few doctors in their communities. Healthcare costs will rise because of the lack of doctors and medical facilities.
>
> In a 2009 poll by the Christian Medical Association, 20% of medical students reported that they are "not pursuing a career in Obstetrics or Gynecology" because of perceived discrimination and coercion in their field. This is a serious problem.

Without future faith-based medical professionals and medical facilities, millions of Americans will not be able to receive the quality medical care they need. It is critical that medical professionals continue to have proper protections in order to serve women across the country.

• In April 2009, Obama delivered a speech at Georgetown, a Catholic university run by the Jesuit order. Curiously missing from behind the school's podium as Obama spoke was the customary monogram symbolizing the name of Jesus Christ. The reason for its absence: Obama's aides had put pressure on the school to conceal the religious image.

• In the spring of 2009, it was reported that the Obama administration had insulted the Vatican by floating the names of three supporters of abortion rights as potential U.S. ambassadors to the Holy See. Obama finally settled on Miguel H. Diaz, nominating him in May 2009. Diaz is known as a liberal Catholic—with sympathies for politicized liberation theology, which is opposed by the Vatican—who taught at St. John's University and the College of Saint Benedict, among other schools. Diaz had served on Obama's sham "Catholic advisory board" during the 2008 campaign. Diaz was also one of twenty-six Catholics who signed a letter of support after Kathleen Sebelius, a dissident Catholic who asserts a right to abortion and contraception, was nominated to head up the Department of Health and Human Services.

Obama's first trip to the Vatican later that year was equally awkward. Obama used the occasion to repay an ailing Ted Kennedy for his support in 2008 by handing Pope Benedict XVI a letter from the Massachusetts senator. The exchange bordered on parody: Obama gave Pope Benedict a letter from the most notorious pro-abortion Catholic in the United States Senate; Pope Benedict gave Obama the pro-life document *Dignitas Personae* (Pope Benedict also gave him his encyclical, *Caritas in Veritate*).

Obama seemed befuddled by the swap, saying the papal gifts would give him something to read on his short flight to Ghana. After Obama's departure, the Vatican released a statement saying the Holy Father had spoken to Obama about abortion and religious freedom: "[the meeting] turned first of all to questions which are in the interests of all and which constitute a great challenge for the future of every nation and for the true progress of peoples, such as the defense and promotion of life and the right to abide by one's conscience."

• In April 2009, it was revealed that Secretary Janet Napolitano's Department of Homeland Security had produced a report on "right-wing extremism." One of the possible threats to America's national security was, allegedly, the potential for rampant pro-life terrorism: "Rightwing extremism in the United States can be broadly divided into those groups, movements, and adherents that are primarily hate-oriented (based on hatred of particular religious, racial or ethnic groups), and those that are mainly antigovernment, rejecting federal authority in favor of state or local authority, or rejecting government authority entirely. It may include groups and individuals that are dedicated to a single issue, such as opposition to abortion or immigration."

The thrust of the report was that opponents of Obama might easily become right-wing extremists, and among those potential opponents are those who believe in a right to life. Such propaganda was useful to Obama, as it is easier to stifle the free speech and religious freedom of pro-lifers if an official-looking "report" from the Department of Homeland Security identifies them as a potential terrorist threat. Of course, the report rested on a lie: that pro-lifers are sowing violence rather than trying to stop it. Surgical abortion, by any rational definition, is the infliction of deadly force—of violence—to prevent the birth of a baby. It would have made more sense for Napolitano to list Obama's abortionist allies at Planned Parenthood as an extremist group.

• In May 2009, Obama dropped his predecessor's practice of holding a public event at the White House to commemorate the National Day of Prayer. In keeping with his notion of religion as a purely private matter, Obama observed the day behind closed doors. Or so his then-press spokesman Robert Gibbs explained: "That's the way the president will publicly observe National Prayer Day. Privately he'll pray as he does every day."

Religious leaders found Obama's scotching of a public event at the White House perplexing. "We are disappointed at the lack of emphasis on prayer at the National Day of Prayer," James Dobson of Focus on the Family said to the press after hearing Gibbs's announcement. "When the professional baseball team wins the World Series, or when the Super Bowl is played, or when college teams win the national championship, they are invited to the White House to celebrate. That's important, apparently, but celebrating prayer, which is our heritage, is ignored."

Indeed, the White House has hosted a steady stream of superficial celebrities. But Obama couldn't find time in his schedule to invite pastors to mark the National Day of Prayer.

Naturally, prominent secularists and leaders of the secularly inclined religious left applauded the president for his decision. "The president is required by federal law to declare a National Day of Prayer, but there is no requirement that a special event be held at the White House in observance of this event," said the Reverend Barry Lynn, the executive director of Americans United for Separation of Church and State.

• In May 2009, Obama delighted secularists by proposing a plan to phase out the District of Columbia's voucher program, the vast majority of whose beneficiaries went to Catholic parochial schools. Denying these children the chance to attend Catholic schools their parents couldn't otherwise afford was more important to Obama than offering them greater educational opportunity. He also wanted to reward the powerful teachers' unions, which had been clamoring for the program's death.

The program was a potential lifeline for poor parents who wanted to remove their children from D.C.'s intellectually dismal and morally bankrupt public schools. Religious leftists helped Obama pull the plug on the program and then badmouthed it as Republicans sought to restore funding. "Though religious schools provide an important service to many students and families, public funds should not go to private religious schools or to any educational institutions that may discriminate against students and teachers based on religion," said the Reverend Welton Gaddy, president of the Interfaith Alliance. Never mind that "discrimination" was not the issue for parents; it was only an issue for the teachers' unions, because Catholic school teachers aren't unionized. Reverend Barry Lynn, a regular collaborator with the secularists, called the voucher program a "$100 million congressional giveaway to religious and other private schools"—better the money be wasted, apparently, in the failing public schools—and said it "was not going to help reduce the budget deficit."

A president who added millions of dollars in "family planning" to his failed and wasteful trillion dollar "Stimulus" bill couldn't spare any money for inner city D.C. parents desperate to give their children a future.

• In May 2009, Obama eliminated all funding for abstinence-only sex education. He put in its place tens of millions of dollars in funding for "comprehensive sexual education." By July 2010, he had spent $190 million on sex education, according to the online publication *Salon*.

The result is that virtually all students in the United States are required to receive state-sponsored sexual education from elementary school through high school, and the operative assumption is that it is right for the state to tell students how to have sex outside marriage—

a sin in the eyes of traditional Christians and Jews. According to the state-sponsored sex education orthodoxy, using artificial birth control—which faithful Catholics regard as contrary to God's will—is an acceptable and proper way to enjoy "safe sex." Obama's order was a reminder of something we all too easily forget: the secular state is imposing on the American people, through sex education and other forms of state propaganda, its own version of sexual morality, which is opposed to traditional Judeo-Christian sexual morality.

• In May 2009, Obama nominated Kevin Jennings, a gay rights activist who had condoned pederasty, to head up the Department of Education's Office of Safe and Drug-Free Schools. Dubbed Obama's "Safe Schools Czar," Jennings said that he had been "inspired" by the gay rights activist Harry Hay, a supporter of the North American Man Boy Love Association. News of Jennings's views outraged religious parents across the country.

Jennings is, of course, an outspoken opponent of the "religious right," quoted in one speech as saying, "We have to quit being afraid of the religious right.... I'm trying not to say, '[F---] 'em!' which is what I want to say, because I don't care what they think! Drop dead!"

Jennings is the founder of the Gay, Lesbian, Straight Education Network (GLSEN), a homosexual activist group that now has thousands of chapters at high schools across the country. GLSEN chapters and materials have promoted sex between young teens and adults and sponsored "field trips" to gay pride parades. Jennings was the keynote speaker at a notorious GLSEN conference at Tufts University in 2000 at which HIV/AIDS coordinators discussed in detail, before an audience which included high school students, matters pertaining to anal and oral sodomy.

In the 2008 campaign, Obama's critics charged that he supported Planned Parenthood's goal of subjecting elementary school students to its sex education propaganda. Obama heatedly denied the charge after John McCain's campaign operatives ran a damaging ad advancing the claim. Obama's critics were proven right by the Jennings appointment.

Jennings wrote the foreword to a book called *Queering Elementary Education*, wherein he asserted that "We must address antigay bigotry...as soon as students start going to school." Jennings held that all schools should be required to include LGBT [lesbian, gay, bisexual, transgender] themes in their curricula.

Obama's Education secretary, Arne Duncan, defended Jennings after it came out that he had once offered glib and immoral counsel to a student who reported to him having had sex with an adult. In a 2000 talk before a GLSEN audience, Jennings admitted that he told a "15-year-old" who confided in him about this incident of pederasty, "I hope you knew to use a condom."

At least fifty-three members of Congress, appalled by this story, called on Obama to fire Jennings as the head of the Office of Safe and Drug-Free Schools. They cited Jennings's "self-described history of ignoring the sexual abuse of a child." The letter also noted that in Jennings's own memoir he describes his "use of illegal drugs without expressing regret or acknowledging the devastating effect illegal drug use can have."

Arne Duncan ignored this letter and praised Jennings. He is "uniquely qualified for his job, and I am honored to have him on our team," said Duncan.

Obama's top educator is a champion of gay rights himself. In May 2012, not long after Vice President Joe Biden had blurted out his support for "men marrying men and women marrying women" on NBC's *Meet the Press*, Duncan endorsed gay marriage on national television. In Illinois, Duncan is famous for having tried to start a "gay high school" in Chicago. Obama's selection of Duncan to head up the Department of Education was no accident. Gay activists who see public schools as the principal means of controlling the moral and religious views of the young had lobbied Obama to name Duncan to the post so as to ensure that their propaganda would flood the country.

Even in liberal Chicago, Duncan's plans for a high school designed to accommodate gay students was seen as outré. In proposing this ludicrous plan, Duncan was trying to capitalize on the politically correct panic over gay teen suicides. He explained that his proposed gay high school would protect students against sneers and bullying, and he vowed that at least half of the student body would be composed of students identified as lesbian, gay, bisexual, or "transgender."

Then-Chicago Mayor Richard Daley, typically a supporter of gay and lesbian causes, declined to back Duncan's scheme. Duncan planned to call his crackpot innovation the Social Justice Solidarity High School, but the school board balked and his proposal was withdrawn.

Religious parents should keep in mind that Arne Duncan is Barack Obama's idea of a cutting-edge educator and moral tutor to the young. Nor should they forget that Kevin Jennings is Obama's idea of a "Safe Schools Czar."

• In July 2009, Obama extended federal benefits to the same-sex partners of government employees, Executive Branch officials, and Foreign Service officers abroad—an egregious violation of the law of the land as established by the federal Defense of Marriage Act (DOMA). At his inauguration, Obama promised to uphold all laws; he clearly didn't mean DOMA.

The *Washington Post*, a reliable champion of gay rights, immediately saw the significance of the move, running three stories the day after the directive was issued. The *Post* noted that the gay-centric policy "does not cover domestic heterosexual partners," and that it had been engineered by John Berry, director of the Office of Personnel Management, who is "the highest-ranking openly gay person in the administration." One of the novel benefits Berry concocted was that gay federal workers could henceforth take time off to care for "children not related by blood or adoption."

• In September 2009, Obama appointed Chai Feldblum to be a commissioner for the Equal Employment Opportunity Commission. Feldblum, a self-described "radical" activist for gay causes, holds that the state has an absolute right to violate the religious freedom of Americans who view homosexual behavior as contrary to the will of God.

"Just as we do not tolerate private racial beliefs that adversely affect African-Americans in the commercial arena, even if such beliefs are based on religious views, we should similarly not tolerate private beliefs about sexual orientation and gender identity that adversely affect LGBT [lesbian, gay, bisexual, and transgender] people," Feldblum wrote in a 2006 *Brooklyn Law Review* article entitled "Moral Conflict and Liberty: Gay Rights and Religion."

Feldblum called the conflict between the freedom of homosexuals and the freedom of the religious a "zero sum game" in which "a gain for one side necessarily entails a corresponding loss for the other side." In this game, the state should see to it that the religious side loses, she wrote.

"For those who believe that a homosexual or bisexual orientation is not morally neutral, and that an individual who acts on his or her homosexual orientation is acting in a sinful or harmful manner (to himself or herself and to others), it is problematic when the government passes a law that gives such individuals equal access to all societal institutions," she explained. "Conversely, for those who believe that any sexual orientation, including a homosexual or bisexual orientation, is morally neutral, and that an individual who acts on his or her homosexual or bisexual orientation acts in an honest and good manner, it is problematic when the government *fails* to pass laws providing equality to such individuals."

Religion, she wrote, should have "no relevance" to the state as it referees this game. "Belief liberty," as she put it, must give way to the "identity liberty" of homosexuals: "Protecting one group's identity liberty may, at times, require that we burden others' belief liberty. This is an inherent and irreconcilable reality of our complex society."

Continuing this point, Feldblum added: "I believe it is essential that we not privilege moral beliefs that are religiously based over other sincerely held core, moral beliefs. Laws passed pursuant to public policies may burden the belief liberty of those who adhere to either religious or secular beliefs."

Of course, the key question is: If traditional religious or moral values are not to guide law, what is to guide it? If the secular state is to impose its values and deny the people's "belief liberty," on what will the state base its values? This is the real revolutionary thrust of modern liberalism and of the Obama administration: it is the creation of a new, mandatory, state-enforced secularism.

Obama understands that the greatest social revolutions are engineered not against state power but with it. The Chai Feldblums are his commissars in his state-sanctioned revolution against religion.

• In October 2009, Obama signed a defense authorization bill into which "hate crimes" legislation had been snuck—a provision that gay activists have long pushed as part of their campaign to muzzle pastors critical of homosexual behavior.

In floor debate during the Senate's deliberations on the bill, Senator Jim DeMint of South Carolina argued that it amounted to "thought crimes" legislation aimed at silencing Christians. He warned that America was moving toward Canada's system of fining politically incorrect views. DeMint referenced the case of a youth pastor, Stephen Boissoin, who was fined $7,000 by the Alberta Human Rights Commission for simply writing a letter to a local newspaper in which he described homo-sexual behavior as sinful.

"Canadians right now live under this kind of regime, where so-called human rights commissions operating outside the normal legal process prosecute citizens for espousing opinions the commissioners disagree with. Today in the United States only actions are crimes," said DeMint. "If we pass this conference report, opinions will become crimes. What is to stop us from following the lead of the European countries and American college campuses where certain speech is criminalized? Can priests, pastors and rabbis be sure their preaching will not be prosecuted if it says certain things are right and wrong?"

Obama's "hate crimes" bill passed.

• In April 2010, the son of Billy Graham, Franklin Graham, was disinvited from the Pentagon's National Day of Prayer event after Obama officials caved in to complaints from a politically correct watchdog group called the Military Religious Freedom Foundation about his "Islamophobia." Graham, like all orthodox Christians since the seventh century, has taken issue with the theology of Islam, but he bears no ill will toward individual Muslims. "It's a part of the world I love very much," Graham told CNN, referring to the people of Muslim countries. "And I understand it. But I certainly disagree with their teaching."

This was enough for Obama's military to insult Billy Graham's son and subject him to a patronizing lecture on acceptable religious views. Army spokesman Colonel Tom Collins felt free to judge the theological value of Graham's comments about Islam. They were "not appropriate," he told the press. "We're an all-inclusive military. We honor all faiths.... Our message to our service and civilian work force is about the need for diversity and appreciation of all faiths." Apparently that "appreciation" does not include talk about how they might differ.

As we will report in a later chapter, orthodox Christian pastors and priests are simply not welcome in Obama's military. Islam fits Obama's liberal paradigm of an oppressed minority to be protected. Jews and Christians—who are targeted by militant Muslims around the world—do not.

• In July 2010, the Obama administration used taxpayer funds to impose the propaganda of Planned Parenthood and other pro-abortion groups on Kenyans. State Department busybodies pressed the African country to include "reproductive rights" in its new constitution. Congressman Chris Smith of New Jersey, drawing upon a report by the U.S. Agency for International Development, complained that more than $23 million in U.S. taxpayer funds had been spent on pushing this constitutional referendum in Kenya. Smith contends that such expenditures violate the Siljander Amendment, a federal law that bans abortion lobbying by the U.S. government in foreign lands.

Kenyans did not forget the insult of their distant kinsman's interference. In May 2012, after Obama endorsed gay marriage, the Kenyan Council of Imams and Preachers launched a bitter attack on him. The Organizing Secretary of the group, Sheikh Mohammed Khalifa, accused Obama of usurping the authority of God by legalizing what "God Himself objects."

"Simply because he has risen to be the President of a superpower does not mean he can now start acting as God. He is nothing in the eyes of God and his plans will not succeed just like those who preceded him in such plans," according to Sheikh Khalifa. "God created man and woman so that we can procreate. How come we now want to behave worse than dogs…?"

Obama's meddling in Kenyan affairs is apparently his attempt to fulfill the "dreams" of his father, a Marxist who sought to replace bourgeois morality with socialism and secularism.

• By October 2010, reporters had begun to notice that Obama no longer included the phrase, "their Creator," in his use of quotations from the Declaration of Independence.

The document says: "We hold these truths to be self-evident, that all men are created equal, that they are endowed by their Creator with certain unalienable rights, that among these are Life, Liberty, and the Pursuit of Happiness." On multiple occasions, Obama changed the line to read: "We hold these truths to be self-evident, that all men are created equal, that each of us are endowed with certain inalienable rights, that among these are life, liberty and the pursuit of happiness."

• On November 10, 2010, Obama comically botched the nation's official motto—which is "In God We Trust"—during a speech on Islam at the University of Indonesia in Jakarta. An apparently confused Obama coined a new one. "In the United States, our motto is E pluribus unum— out of many, one," he said.

Irate members of Congress pointed this error out to White House officials. But they refused to issue a correction. When these same congressmen proposed a resolution reaffirming "In God We Trust" as the official U.S. motto, Obama publicly belittled them for it.

• In February 2011, Obama still hadn't filled the State Department post for the ambassador who monitors religious persecution around the world. Doug Bandow, writing in the *Washington Times*, noted that Obama's eventual nominee, a motivational speaker and theologically liberal female minister, had no real qualifications for the job:

> ...religious liberty appears to be an almost nonexistent priority for this administration...the U.S. national security strategy didn't even mention religious freedom as a "value." Not

until June 15—nearly 15 months after he took office—did the president nominate the ambassador-at-large, and he did so only after public prodding by the House International Religious Freedom Caucus, among others.... Mr. Obama's nominee, the Rev. Suzan D. Johnson Cook, has no obvious qualifications for the job. Although she is talented, her past work has not involved international religious freedom. She has no known diplomatic experience. Her nomination appears to be intended to satisfy domestic constituencies—for instance, she was an adviser on President Clinton's Domestic Policy Council. Equally worrisome is that the administration has further diminished the Office of International Religious Freedom bureaucratically. If confirmed—though there is skepticism about her nomination, it is not clear there will be outright opposition—Ms. Cook will report to the assistant secretary for democracy, human rights and labor, not the secretary of state. Moreover, the office's employees will be largely out of her control.

Cook has struggled to make any impact with the job. To take one example, she had plans to visit China, a notorious abuser of religious freedom, in February 2012. But those plans were ditched after China denied her a visa. "We look forward to traveling and looking at a mutually agreeable time when it works for China and it works for us," said Cook weakly after the snub.

• In February 2011, Obama instructed his Justice Department to abandon any defense of the federal Defense of Marriage Act—an abdication of the law, which created space for the federal government to operate on the issue of gay marriage by presidential edict rather than by congressional legislation. Gregory Kane, an African-American columnist for the

Washington Examiner, looking back at this policy of unapologetic lawlessness in the light of Obama's endorsement of gay marriage in 2012, wrote scathingly,

> By having the Justice Department refuse to defend DOMA, Obama in essence is telling Americans that he will choose which laws his administration will enforce, and which ones it won't.
>
> At his 2009 inauguration, Obama swore to uphold the laws of the United States. Many of us saw and/or heard him take that oath.
>
> I'm sure none of us heard Obama say, "I will uphold and enforce all laws, except the Defense of Marriage Act." Obama was "frontin'" for three years about his views on gay marriage. Apparently, he was "frontin'" when he took his oath of office too.

• In early April 2011, Obama endorsed ENDA, the Employment Non-Discrimination Act, legislation gay activists had pushed in the hopes of punishing employers who object to hiring the "transgendered" or homosexuals. ENDA, argued Indiana Congressman Mike Pence at the time, "wages war on freedom of religion in the workplace." The aforementioned gay rights activist Chai Feldblum was one of ENDA's architects.

• In July 2011, it was reported that veterans in Texas were upset that Obama's Department of Veterans Affairs had banned any mention of Jesus Christ during burials at Houston National Cemetery. According to the *Houston Chronicle*, hundreds of demonstrators turned out on Independence Day at the cemetery to support a lawsuit against the ban. After these and other protests, the ban was lifted.

• In August 2011, the *Washington Post* reported that the Air Force cancelled a course on Just War theory, deeming the theory's philosophical origins to be too Christian and biblical: "Air Force suspends ethics course that used Bible passages to train missile launch officers," read a headline in the *Washington Post*.

The course on Just War theory had been taught for more than twenty years. All it took to kill the longstanding course was a momentary blast of secularist mau-mauing by the usual left-wing suspects. Truthout.org, a liberal website, had received documents from the mis-named Military Religious Freedom Foundation which showed—brace yourselves—that the course made mention of such religious figures as Abraham, John the Baptist, and Saint Augustine, one of the most famous articulators of Just War theory. One supposedly offensive presentation mentioned "many examples of believers engaged in wars in the Old Testament" and noted the absence of "pacifistic sentiment in mainstream Jewish history."

Once again, Obama's politicized military caved in to an absurd complaint. David Smith, a spokesman for the Air Force's Air Education and Training Command, told the press that "senior leadership looked at [the material for the course] and said, no, we could do better than this."

In interviews with reporters, Mikey Weinstein, president of the secularist Military Religious Freedom Foundation, hailed the course's demise as a victory for the separation of church and state. No longer would soldiers have to hear the "Jesus loves nukes speech," as one of his offended clients put it.

• In September 2011, the Army revised guidelines for Walter Reed Medical Center to read: "No religious items (i.e. Bibles, reading materials and/or facts) are allowed to be given away or used during a visit." The hospital rescinded this policy after Congressman Steve King drew attention to it on the House floor. "That means you can't bring in a Bible and read from it when you visit your son or your daughter, perhaps—or your wife or husband," King said. "It means a priest that might be coming in to visit someone on their deathbed couldn't bring in the Eucharist, couldn't offer Last Rites. This is the most outrageous affront."

Embarrassed officials at Walter Reed dropped the policy. But King was shocked that the policy had even been contemplated. "I don't think there's any excuse for it and there's no talking it away," King said to Fox News after the policy was reversed. "The very existence of this, whether it's enforced or not, tells you what kind of a mindset is there."

"The idea that these soldiers, sailors, airmen and Marines that have fought to defend our Constitution, and that includes our First Amendment rights to religious liberty—would be denied that religious liberty when they are lying in a hospital bed recovering from wounds incurred while defending that liberty is the most bitter and offensive type of an irony that I can think of," he continued.

• In September 2011, Obama, yet again defying the federal Defense of Marriage Act, ordered the Pentagon to authorize the performance of same-sex marriage ceremonies on military bases.

• In November 2011, Obama again neglected any mention of God in his Thanksgiving address, the day on which the country remembers the pilgrims who fled to America in the hope of exercising religious freedom, the day which commemorates that first feast in 1621 at which the pilgrims gave thanks to God for safely guiding them to the New World to find religious freedom.

• In November 2011, the Air Force Academy ended its support for Operation Christmas Child, a charity that distributes gifts to needy children across the world, on the grounds that a Christian group headed up by Franklin Graham was running it. The Military Religious Freedom

Foundation succeeded again in scaring the military into dropping a commendable program.

"Operation Christmas Child said they expect to send more than 8 million shoe box gifts to underprivileged children in 100 countries. Around 60,000 churches and 60,000 community groups in the United States are participating," reported Fox News. "Mikey Weinstein, of the Military Religious Freedom Foundation, said an evangelical Christian message is also included in the boxes. 'This is a proselytizing entity of Franklin Graham,' said... Weinstein. He filed a complaint on behalf of 132 Academy personnel including two sets of Muslim-American parents."

"It's so outrageous," said Jordan Sekulow, an attorney with the American Center for Law and Justice, to Fox News. "This is a perfect example of how heartless these groups are when it comes to defending their anti-religion position. It's not about the First Amendment. It's about a real hatred of religious people and people of faith that they would go so far as to stop an assistance program like Operation Christmas Child."

• In November 2011, the House of Representatives investigated charges that the Obama administration, in its selection of grant recipients, had been discriminating against Catholic institutions. The majority on the House Oversight and Government Reform Committee concluded that Obama had grossly discriminated against the Catholic Church. The committee focused in particular on the Obama administration's mysterious pulling of a longstanding grant from the Catholic bishops for work that helps the victims of sex trafficking.

The Obama administration's decision to pull the grant was so politicized and dubious that even some Health and Human Services staffers had opposed it. These staffers told the press that HHS Secretary Kathleen Sebelius was simply punishing the Church for refusing to dispense contraceptives and abortifacients to prostitutes and other victims of sex trafficking.

As the *Washington Post* reported:

> In the case of the trafficking contract, senior political appoin-
> tees at HHS stepped in to award the new grants to the bishops'
> competitors, overriding an independent review board and
> career staffers who had recommended that the bishops be
> funded again, according to federal officials and internal HHS
> documents.... The decision not to fund the bishops this time
> has caused controversy inside HHS. A number of career offi-
> cials refused to sign documents connected to the grant, feeling
> that the process was unfair and politicized, individuals famil-
> iar with the matter said. Their concerns have been reported
> to the HHS inspector general's office.

The *Post* continued:

> HHS policies spell out that career officials usually oversee
> grant competitions and select the winners, giving priority
> consideration to the review board's judgment. The policies do
> not prohibit political appointees from getting involved,
> though current and former employees said it is unusual, espe-
> cially for high-level officials.

Sister Mary Ann Walsh, an official at the United States Conference of
Catholic Bishops, wrote on the bishops' website that "there seems to be
a new unwritten reg at the U.S. Department of Health and Human Services (HHS). It's the ABC Rule, Anybody But Catholics. The program
worked well on the ground, but not so well for distant administrators
promoting the abortion and contraceptive agenda, who bristle at the fact
that in accord with Church teaching, USCCB won't facilitate taking
innocent life, sterilization and artificial contraception."

• In early December 2011, the Obama administration unfurled a bizarre new mission for the State Department: the promotion of gay rights abroad, including in religious countries that regard homosexual behavior as sinful.

Obama's secretary of State, Hillary Clinton, used a speech in Geneva, Switzerland, to lecture reluctant countries about "Lesbian, Gay, Bisexual, and Transgender Rights." She informed them that "LGBT rights" now form a "priority of our foreign policy."

She conveniently ignored that many Islamic countries—with whom Obama proudly says that "America is not at war"—still maintain anti-sodomy laws. Presumably those countries are exempt from this campaign.

Clinton said in the speech that she had instructed U.S. diplomats to operate like gay rights activists abroad, and that she was outfitting embassies with activism "toolkits":

> In our embassies, our diplomats are raising concerns about specific cases and laws, and working with a range of partners to strengthen human rights protections for all....In Washington, we have created a task force at the State Department to support and coordinate this work. And in the coming months, we will provide every embassy with a toolkit to help improve their efforts. And we have created a program that offers emergency support to defenders of human rights for LGBT people.

She also announced that the American taxpayer would be picking up the bill for a new "Global Equality Fund," which advances propaganda in favor of Lesbian-Gay-Bisexual-Transgendered (LGBT) activism.

The Founding Fathers would surely have been surprised to learn that promoting gay marriage and sex-change operations overseas constitutes a "priority of U.S. foreign policy."

In laying out her bumptious case for inalienable "LGBT" rights that transcend and therefore bind all foreign governments, Hillary Clinton made no mention of where these rights originate. She cryptically said that governments don't grant rights, but did not cite "our Creator" as their source, perhaps sensing that it was best to leave God out of Obama's ambition to impose the secular progressive view on the whole world.

An administration that came to power calling George W. Bush a bully who sought to impose Western ideology on foreign countries feels entitled to impose "LGBT" rights on Catholic, Islamic, Hindu, Buddhist, and Jewish ones.

In her Geneva remarks, Hillary Clinton singled out for a browbeating countries that see homosexual behavior as sinful. She scolded them for regarding it as a "Western phenomenon."

This initiative is not the only Obama-directed State Department attempt to undercut religion and traditional morality abroad. In his first term, Obama has also been pushing ratification of the UN Treaty on Women. This treaty would require us to "modify the social and cultural patterns of conduct of men and women," to follow UN dictates about "family education," to revise our textbooks to conform to feminist ideology in order to ensure "the elimination of any stereotyped concept of the roles of men and women," and to set up a federal "network of child-care facilities." Like all UN treaties, the UN Treaty on Women creates a monitoring commission of so-called "experts" to force compliance. The monitors of this Treaty on Women have already singled out Mother's Day as a stereotype that must be eliminated and criticized Slovenia because "less than 30 percent of children under three years of age were in formal day care."

Another UN treaty on Obama's wish list is the UN Treaty on the Rights of the Child, which was signed in 1995 by Bill Clinton but never ratified by the Senate. This is a pet project of statists who believe that the "village" (that is, the government or UN "experts"), rather than parents, should raise children. This treaty would give children rights against their parents so that they could express their own views "freely in all matters," receive information of all kinds through "media of the child's choice," and would grant them a right to "rest and leisure." The treaty even orders schools to teach respect for the "Charter of the United Nations."

• In February 2012, Audrey Hudson reported for *Human Events* that "the federal government will no longer forgive student loans in exchange for public service if that service is related to religion, according to a new Education Department rule."

Hudson reported a portion of the rule:

> Generally, the type or nature of employment with the organization does not matter for PSLF [Public Service Loan Forgiveness] purposes. However, if you work for a nonprofit organization, your employment will not qualify for PSLF if your job duties are related to religious instruction, worship services, or any form of proselytizing.

• In February 2012, the Air Force, responding to complaints from the Military Association of Atheists and Freethinkers, removed the Latin word for God, Dei, from the logo of the Rapid Capabilities Office (RCO). Congressman Randy Forbes from Virginia called on the Air Force to reverse its "egregious" decision.

The logo for the Rapid Capabilities Office originally carried the motto, "Opus Dei Cum Pecunia Alienum Efficemus" ("Doing God's Work with Other People's Money"). The new logo says: "Miraculi Cure Pecunia Alienum Efficemus" ("Doing Miracles with Other People's Money"). The change left atheists still unhappy, as they object to the word miracles too.

Thirty-six members of Congress, led by Forbes, sent a letter to Air Force Chief of Staff General Norton Schwartz to protest the change. "The action taken by the RCO suggests that all references to God, regardless of their context, must be removed from the military. We ask that you reverse this perplexing decision." Forbes added to the press that he considered it part of "a disturbing trend of inaccuracies and omissions, misunderstandings of church and state, rogue court challenges and efforts to remove God from the public domain by unelected bureaucrats."

• In February 2012, the Army warned Catholic chaplains not to read from a letter decrying the HHS contraceptive/abortifacient mandate—a letter that Archbishop Timothy Broglio, head of the military services archdiocese, had asked the chaplains to read.

This list could be expanded, but these examples should give readers some sense of the breadth and depth of the Obama administration's hostility to religion.

CHAPTER FOUR

THE GREAT CON

O bama has learned from the past. He knows that to achieve his secularist aims—to make government the national arbiter of morality, to subordinate religious freedom to government coercion—he needs to cloak them in the guise of faith.

In 2004, Democratic Party presidential nominee John Kerry, a liberal Catholic, ceded "values voters" to evangelical George W. Bush, and he paid the price for it.

Rejecting the cynical advice of former president Bill Clinton (who now supports gay marriage) that he endorse a traditional marriage proposition in the crucial Midwestern bellwether state of Ohio, Kerry refused to take a stand on that question. He told aides that following Clinton's advice would have made him look "intolerant." Kerry lost Ohio and the election.

In the wake of Kerry's defeat, Democrats panned the Massachusetts liberal for failing to appeal to churchgoing Americans. "Democrats did not connect well enough with the American people," Congresswoman Nancy Pelosi told CNN, taking a swipe at Kerry. "Certainly Democrats are faith-filled. Certainly we love our country, and we're very patriotic, but somehow or other that did not come across when 61% of those who are regular churchgoers voted Republican—voted for President Bush, and when 22% of Americans gave its highest number to what determined their vote to issues relating to morality, more than the economy, more than terrorism."

"I believe that we have it within us," she exhorted fellow Democrats. "I know that many of the people who are in politics on the Democratic side do so according to the—the gospel of Matthew and indeed the Bible, but we don't demonstrate it clearly enough and faith is such an important part of the lives of most people in our country. They want to know that we identify with that."

After spending decades trying to pry the Ten Commandments off the walls of courthouses, after years of seeking to remove God from the pledge of allegiance, after years of denying public money to faith-based charities and harassing upright groups like the Boy Scouts, it took a lot of gall for Pelosi-led Democrats to rebuke Kerry for an insufficient commitment to religious values. Still, Pelosi's exhortation marked a strategic turning point for the Democrats. It signaled a new tone and tack that Barack Obama would seek to exploit four years later.

Obama sought to portray himself as a "new Democrat," one who could talk about religion freely and without embarrassment. Thus began his great con of churchgoing Americans.

Through speeches and posturing, candidate Obama worked hard to gull the religious into voting for him by giving a religious patina to his policies, particularly his opposition to the Iraq War. He "valued" religion, as he put it. He particularly valued the votes of the religious. On his 2008 campaign web page, "people of faith" enjoyed their own special slot, a mere two tabs down from the "Lesbian, Gay, Bisexual and Transgender community."

Obama cast himself as a "post-partisan" politician on matters of faith. He quickly found useful idiots in the religious community to provide him with pulpits and platforms for faux-pensive addresses on religion in politics. Obama shrewdly sensed the possibilities of poaching values voters from the Republican Party by adopting a tone of religious uplift and couching his policies in terms of the Golden Rule.

Obama's duplicitous though effective outreach to religious voters benefited from another factor: the leftward drift of religion in America since the 1960s, which has created what author Ross Douthat provocatively calls "a nation of heretics." In modern America, secularism is like an acid that burns through everything it touches, including religion. Obama hoped to exploit this phenomenon, which can be seen in measurable "generational change" among younger Protestants. As pollsters for the *Religion & Ethics Newsweekly* and the United Nations Foundation discovered, young Protestants have, for example, adopted "a more inclusive definition of what it means to be 'pro-life' and are more supportive of efforts to combat global warming."

Obama enlisted religious supporters who accepted his progressive liberalism as faith-based and in accord with Christian values. The ostensibly pro-life Catholic law professor Doug Kmiec, who would later receive an ambassadorship to Malta from Obama, churned out articles claiming that Obama was more "pro-life" than John McCain, despite the Democratic candidate's 100 percent voting rating from pro-abortion groups like Planned Parenthood. Archbishop Charles Chaput called Kmiec's brazen claim a form of "self-hypnosis," but it actually worked: under its spell, a majority of Catholics voted for a candidate who made no secret of his support for the "choice" to kill unborn children, and even, notoriously, "born-alive" ones—babies who survived an abortionist's first attempt to kill them.

Obama made a play for less doctrinaire, secularized Christians by shoehorning libertine liberalism into quasi-Christian concepts and vocabulary—a game that he and his fellow Democrats still play, as evident in their "religious" awakening to gay marriage. Obama now cites the "Golden Rule" as his reason for supporting gay marriage, and Pelosi says, "My religion has, compels me—and I love it for it—to be against discrimination of any kind in our country, and I consider [prohibiting gay marriage] a form of discrimination."

Cynical activists from Saul Alinsky to "chaplains" for Planned Parenthood have long urged elected Democrats to exploit the organizing power of religion for secularist and socialist purposes. Obama has always accepted and acted on that advice, deploying, whenever the opportunity to confuse the faithful presents itself, seductive sophistries and religious-sounding rationalizations. Assuming his most pensive and soulful pose, he mused on the "connection between religion and politics" during the 2008 campaign. But the only real connection between the two for him was strategic. His much-advertised appreciation of "religion in public life" was designed not to purify the party's extreme secularism but to advance it, using the language of religion to win the presidency so that he could marginalize the religious. For Obama, the "connection between religion and politics" was a public relations pitch, not a fundamental alteration to the Democrats' increasingly secularist philosophical biases.

During the 2008 race, fawning journalists dug up a supposedly seminal June 2006 speech on religion in public life that Obama delivered at Call to Renewal's "Building a Covenant for a New America" conference. They purred over it for days. But what of substance had he said in it? On close examination it didn't add up to much. He was essentially tutoring progressives in the value and efficacy of patting the religious on the head from time to time. As he said, "I think we make a mistake when we fail to acknowledge the power of faith in people's lives—in the lives of the

American people—and I think it's time that we join a serious debate about how to reconcile faith with our modern, pluralistic democracy." Or in other words, reconcile faith with liberalism.

Obama affected to explain how Christianity guides his politics. But a close reading of the speech reveals that the influence is all in reverse: his liberal politics guide his Christianity. Doctrinal Christianity is a disposable proposition for him, while political liberalism represents an organizing, not-to-be-doubted-or-changed truth for society. Indeed, liberalism is so obviously true and authoritative that the traditional understanding of Christianity must give way to it, according to Obama's thinking. Though he would never dare question the Koran, he has implied the Bible's condemnation of homosexual behavior is in need of an interpretational overhaul under the light of modern liberalism. Obama appears to assume that while the Bible is a fallible document, the doctrines of modern liberalism are beyond any questioning, which is why he seems so confident, even arrogant, in dismissing his critics. He knows the truth; they represent error and ignorance. For him, secularism is synonymous with "reason" and religion synonymous with "mere opinion," which explains why Obama regards his "evolving" views as infallible and Christianity's changeless principles as disposable.

Obama automatically accepts secular liberal premises and feels no need to defend them. At the same time, however, he sought as a candidate to flatter the religious through patronizing rhetoric. In his 2006 speech on faith and politics, he encouraged the religious to enter public life in a "pluralistic" society, provided that they could aspire to secularism's high level of rationality:

> Democracy demands that the religiously motivated translate their concerns into universal, rather than religion-specific, values. It requires that their proposals be subject to argument,

and amenable to reason. I may be opposed to abortion for religious reasons, but if I seek to pass a law banning the practice, I cannot simply point to the teachings of my church or evoke God's will. I have to explain why abortion violates some principle that is accessible to people of all faiths, including those with no faith at all.

What is interesting here is that Obama cites "universal" values in opposition to "religion-specific" ones. This ignores that the claims of Christianity are indeed universal (the word "catholic" means just that). And while dismissing Christian teaching opposed to abortion, what universal moral principle based upon "reason" does he cite when justifying the right of doctors to scalpel to death unborn children? He treats abortion as an undeniable "universal" value. It would never occur to him that "choice" is nothing more than propaganda from the sect of secularism.

THE AUDACITY OF SECULARISM

Barack Obama had rehearsed his 2008 con-job on the religious in his second memoir, *The Audacity of Hope*, a phrase that came directly from a sermon by Jeremiah Wright. In the book, Obama strains to present himself as a supporter of religion even as he betrays his view of secularism as superior to faith. His discussion of religion in the book is that of the cocky college sophomore who assumes religion might be endearing and personally important but needs to be kept private, while "democratic pluralism" requires the acceptance of infallible secular, liberal truths. Obama uses the Old Testament story of Abraham and Isaac to argue that the Bible is subjectively meaningful but publicly dangerous.

"If God has spoken, then followers are expected to live up to God's edicts, regardless of the consequences. To base one's life on such uncompromising commitments may be sublime; to base our policy making on such commitments would be a dangerous thing," Obama writes. Abraham, he continues, had his subjective "experience" with God, which may have been "true" for him, but from the standpoint of democratic pluralism his behavior made him a very bad citizen indeed: "it is fair to say that if any of us saw a twenty-first-century Abraham raising the knife on the roof of his apartment building, we would call the police; we would wrestle him down; even if we saw him lower the knife at the last minute, we would expect the Department of Children and Family Services to take Isaac away and charge Abraham with child abuse."

Obama summed up his sermon on the "reason" of secularism and the dangerous caprice of religion by saying that the "best we can do is act in accordance with those things that are possible for all of us to know." Obama does not tell us outright in what this lowest-common-denominator of wisdom exactly consists, but we know that it is liberalism, and one of its not-to-be-questioned truths is that while Abraham would be or should be arrested by the Department of Children and Family Services, plunging knives into the necks of unborn children is a "matter between a woman and her doctor."

In the end, Abraham didn't kill Isaac. The same can't be said for multitudes of unborn children under Obama, whose friends at Planned Parenthood have their surgical knives paid for with tax dollars. Moreover, Obama isn't exactly a stalwart and trustworthy opponent of infanticide. Obama's "reason" as a state senator in Illinois led him to waffle on banning it.

Obama acknowledges in *The Audacity of Hope* that Alan Keyes, his maverick Republican opponent in the 2004 Illinois Senate race, had unnerved him by calling his Christianity politicized and phony. "Christ would not vote for Barack Obama," said Keyes, citing Obama's stances in favor of abortion and (then) gay civil unions. "Barack Obama has voted to behave in a way that is inconceivable for Christ to have behaved."

Obama was flustered by Keyes's attack, as he admits in the book:

> I found him getting under my skin in a way that few people
> ever have. When our paths crossed during the campaign, I
> often had to suppress the rather uncharitable urge to either
> taunt him or wring his neck. Once when we bumped into each
> other at an Indian Independence Day parade, I poked him in
> the chest while making a point, a bit of alpha-male behavior
> that I hadn't engaged in since high school and which an obser-
> vant news crew gamely captured; the moment was replayed
> in slow motion on TV that evening. In the three debates that
> were held before the election, I was frequently tongue-tied,
> irritable, and uncharacteristically tense.

Obama allows that supporters found his behavior puzzling, given the
ease with which he was beating Keyes in the polls:

> "Why are you letting this guy give you fits?" they would ask
> me. For them, Mr. Keyes was a kook, an extremist, his argu-
> ments not even worth entertaining. What they didn't under-
> stand was that I could not help but take Mr. Keyes seriously.
> For he claimed to speak for my religion—and although I
> might not like what came out of his mouth, I had to admit
> that some of his views had many adherents within the Chris-
> tian church.

Keyes, in other words, had put his finger on a real problem for
Obama—a problem that dogs him to this day. Symbolically, Obama is
still poking his Christian critics in the chest, via the HHS mandate and
his other anti-religious measures.

DREAMS FROM HIS PASTOR

Obama's great con in 2008 required that he distance himself from his pastor of many years, Jeremiah Wright, from whom he had received instruction in a Marxist version of Christianity called "liberation theology" at Trinity United Church of Christ in Chicago. In *Dreams from My Father*, Obama relates the sermon that he says turned him into a Christian. This sermon by Wright contained no specifically doctrinal Christian content, was rawly political, and took a shot at "white folks." Obama quoted a passage from the sermon:

> It is this world, a world where cruise ships throw away more food in a day than most residents of Port-au-Prince see in a year, where white folks' greed runs a world in need, apartheid in one hemisphere, apathy in another hemisphere.... That's the world! On which hope sits!

Obama claimed that he never heard Wright's infamous "God damn America" sermons, even though Obama had sat in Wright's pews for twenty years. The videos of Obama's self-described spiritual mentor surpass *Saturday Night Live* parodies. As his congregants are hopping up and down and fellow pastors are clapping him on the back, a sashaying Wright allows himself a range of rancid and conspiratorial musings that might have given even Louis Farrakhan pause. The feverish racism reaches its high point of buffoonishness when Wright accuses the so-called first black president, Bill Clinton, of "riding dirty," exploiting the black community as he exploited Monica Lewinsky.

Under great political pressure, a reluctant Obama severed his ties with Wright and his church. He cast Wright as the unhinged relative with which most American families are saddled. He neglected to mention that his addled pastor had presided at his wedding, baptized his children, and given him the title to his second memoir. This is the equivalent of, say, Mitt Romney announcing that David Duke had served as best man at his wedding and coined his campaign slogan.

Obama claimed he would have walked out of the church had he heard Wright's "God damn America" sermons. But go back and look at the videos: none of Obama's fellow congregants look appalled or ready to walk out; they were practically doing somersaults of joy down the aisles. Wright's raise-the-roof racism was his customary style and an immense crowd-pleaser. Obama never saw this in his twenty years of attending his sermons? That is simply not plausible. Even the Wright sermon Obama quotes in *Dreams from My Father* contains a hint of his racism in its reference to "white folks' greed."

The Wright controversy threatened to cement Obama's reputation as a stealth radical, cooler in his temperament than overt radicals but equally committed to their goals. That Obama casually talked on the campaign trail about confiscating the profits of oil companies and bankrupting coal mine owners was no surprise, given that Wright's socialist "liberation theology" had shaped Obama's worldview for over a generation.

Obama survived the controversy, thanks in large part to John McCain's inexplicable refusal to make even passing mention of it on the campaign trail. Such a controversy would have sunk any other "Christian" politician. After all, Obama belonged to a straightforwardly racist church that viewed America with at best suspicion and at worst contempt. The church's official literature during Obama's time there was openly separatist, mirroring the white racism of "separate but equal" almost perfectly. A pressed Wright even used the separate but equal defense in an interview on Fox News, saying that separate does not mean superior. The church's literature touted a "Black Value System" and stated, "We are an African people, and remain 'true to our native land.'"

Obama's sudden displeasure with his pastor's comments was bogus. The truth is that he had indulged casual reverse racism from his friends and family for years, as evidenced by his indifference to his wife's outrageous comment, "As a black man Barack can get shot going to the gas station," and her famous boast that she was finally "proud" of her country after his initial success in the Democratic primaries.

According to Obama biographer David Remnick, Obama's reason for joining Wright's church was not religious but political. "Initially, Obama approached Wright as an organizer," Remnick writes in *The Bridge*. Obama liked Wright's brand of Christianity with its Marxist economics, racist thrust, radical politics, and absence of traditional Christian content. According to Wright, Obama wanted to join a relativistic religion: "His search was: 'I need a faith that doesn't put other people's faiths down, and all I'm hearing about is you're going to hell if you don't believe what I believe.' He didn't hear that from me."

Obama did not want to join a historically Christian black church in Chicago that took traditional Christian doctrines seriously. Rather, he sought out a liberal church that would help him advance his budding political career. Remnick notes that Obama could have joined "Reverend Arthur Brazier's enormous Pentecostal church on the South Side." But he didn't, and Brazier explained to Remnick why Obama didn't join his church:

> Reverend Wright and I are on different levels of Christian perspective. Reverend Wright is more into black liberation, he is more of a humanitarian type who sought to free African-Americans from plantation policies. My view was more on the spiritual side. I was more concerned, as I am today, with people accepting Jesus Christ. Winning souls for Christ. The civil-rights movement was an adjunct; as a Christian, you couldn't close your eyes to the injustice. But

in my opinion the church was not established to do that. It was to win souls for Christ.

Speaking to reporter Edward Klein for his book *The Amateur*, Wright acknowledged again that Obama's interest in his version of Christianity was political. Wright added that he had no idea if Obama is even a believing Christian, and that Obama's only religious knowledge upon meeting him derived from Islam: "You studied Islam, didn't you? And Barack said, 'Yeah, Rev, I studied Islam. But help me understand Christianity, because I already know Islam.'"

Klein asked Wright: "Did you convert Obama from Islam to Christianity?" Wright replied, "That's hard to tell. I think I convinced him that it was okay for him to make a choice in terms of who he believed Jesus is. And I told him it was really okay and not a putdown of the Muslim part of his family or his Muslim friends."

What does it say about the quality of the president's "Christian" faith when the pastor who baptized him doesn't even know if he is a believing Christian?

Wright told Klein that he saw the Obamas as secularists, for whom "church is not their thing":

> And even after Barack and Michelle came to the church their kids weren't raised in the church like you raise other kids in Sunday school. No. Church is not their thing. It never was their thing. Michelle was not the kind of black woman whose momma made her go to church, made her go to Sunday school, made her go to Baptist Young People's Union. She wasn't raised in that kind of environment. So the church was not an integral part of their spiritual lives after they got married. But the church was an integral part of Barack's politics. Because he needed that black base.

Church is still "not their thing." Only on rare occasions do the Obamas attend church services in Washington, D.C., and when they do it is with photographers and television crews in tow. Ronald Reagan also rarely attended church as president, but there was a significant difference. Reagan didn't like all the fuss: the security, the publicity. For Obama, it appears the publicity is the point. The great con continues.

CHAPTER FIVE

SAUL ALINSKY'S DEVILS

B arack Obama's interest in religion is in direct proportion to his ability to manipulate it—a political calculus that he absorbed through his study of the life, thought, and methods of Saul Alinsky, a radical socialist from Chicago who established the Industrial Areas Foundation in the 1940s.

On August 31, 2008, not long after the Democratic National Convention in Colorado, the *Boston Globe* published a remarkable letter written by L. David Alinsky, the son of Saul Alinsky. David Alinsky reveled in the fact that Barack Obama had been a disciple of his late father: "I am proud to see that my father's model for organizing is being applied successfully beyond local community organizing to affect the Democratic campaign in 2008. It is a fine tribute to Saul Alinsky as we approach his 100th birthday."

Confirming that Obama was trained in Chicago according to Saul Alinsky's methods, David Alinsky wrote: "It is an amazingly powerful format, and the method of my late father always works to get the message out and get the supporters on board. When executed meticulously and thoughtfully, it is a powerful strategy for initiating change and making it really happen. Obama learned his lesson well."

The Democratic National Convention was a "perfectly organized event, Saul Alinsky style," wrote David Alinsky. "All the elements were present: the individual stories told by real people of their situations and hardships, the packed-to-the rafters crowd, the crowd's chanting of key phrases and names, the action on the spot of texting and phoning to show instant support and commitment to jump into the political battle, the rallying selections of music, the setting of the agenda by the power people."

David Alinsky had good reason to boast. His father's organizing techniques did more than just help an ostensibly longshot candidate climb a steep path past Hillary Clinton to America's highest office; it has helped Obama radicalize the country from that Olympian chair. Obama's war on religious freedom has been nothing if not Alinskyite in its methods and tactics.

Let us pause here briefly and look at those methods, for the most significant education Barack Obama received, as he noted in his memoirs, was not from Columbia University or Harvard Law School but from his training under Saul Alinsky's system as a "community organizer."

Obama was trained by Alinsky's Industrial Areas Foundation. After completing his training, Obama began to teach workshops on the Alinsky method himself. Moving from community organizer to state level politician, Obama eventually put together a Chicago-style presidential campaign that used Alinskyite methods to defeat decisively the Clinton machine (the Clintons were themselves, ironically, acolytes of Alinsky) and then the McCain-led Republican Party in a dramatic one-two punch.

The Industrial Areas Foundation was founded on the South Side of Chicago in 1940. It nestled under the protective wing of the Democratic political machine, but Alinsky's reach eventually extended all over the country, from New York to California. Hillary Clinton wrote her Wellesley College thesis on Alinsky, who then offered her a job (which she turned down to enroll in Yale Law School).

"The Alinsky ideology and Alinsky concepts of mass organization for power" are not relics of the past but practices of the present. Alinsky died in 1972, but he left behind a cadre of community organizers who had been trained how to carry out the political strategies described in Alinsky's frank and elegantly written book called *Rules for Radicals: A Pragmatic Primer for Realistic Radicals* (originally published by Random House in 1971)—a book that made a deep impression on a young Barack Obama.

The tone of Alinsky's book and its obvious determination to change America into a socialist and secularist collective are made clear by the book's audacious dedication to Satan in its first printing (later editions dropped this dedication):

> Lest we forget at least an over-the-shoulder acknowledgment to the very first radical: from all our legends, mythology, and history (and who is to know where mythology leaves off and history begins—or which is which), the first radical known to man who rebelled against the establishment and did it so effectively that he at least won his own kingdom—Lucifer.

Saul Alinsky's worldview was that the United States is an oppressive and racist society where most people ("the Have-Nots") are the victims of economic injustice with a future of despair. He wanted a radical change of America's social and economic structure, and he planned to achieve that through creating public discontent and moral confusion. His goal was not to arrive at compromise or a peaceful solution; his goal was to crush "the Haves" and level American society.

Alinsky developed concepts to achieve power through mass organization. Organizing was his euphemism for revolution. His 1946 book, *Reveille for Radicals*, had already made clear that he wanted to move the United States from capitalism to socialism, where the means of production would be owned by all "the people" (the government). A believer in economic determinism, he viewed unemployment, disease, crime, and bigotry as byproducts of capitalism. So he called for massive change.

To achieve this, he sought local community organizers who projected confidence and vision, and who could offer hope and promises of change. Barack Obama fit this profile perfectly. Alinsky didn't want just talkers; he wanted radicals who were prepared to take bold action to organize the discontented, precipitate crises, grab power, and thereby transform society. He taught these radicals how to infiltrate existing institutions, like churches, unions, and political parties, gain influence in them, and then gradually transform them into instruments of socialist revolution.

RULES FOR RADICALS

Chapter one of *Rules for Radicals*, called "The Purpose," made Alinsky's goal explicitly clear. His worldview holds that mankind is divided into three parts: "the Haves, the Have-Nots, and the Have-a-Little, Want Mores." His purpose is to teach the Have-Nots how to take power and money away from the Haves. "We are concerned," he said, "with how to create mass organizations to seize power.... We are talking about a mass power organization which will change the world.... This means revolution."

"Change" was Alinsky's favorite word, incessantly repeated page after page. "I will argue," he writes, "that man's hopes lie in the acceptance of the great law of change." Alinsky uses what he calls "general concepts of change" to move us toward "a science of revolution."

"Change" meant massive change in our socio-economic structure and culture. What he called "organizing" meant pursuing confrontational political tactics. Alinsky taught the Have-Nots to "hate the establishment of the Haves" because they have "power, money, food, security, and luxury. They suffocate in their surpluses while the Have-Nots starve." He claimed that "justice, morality, law, and order, are mere words used by the Haves to justify and secure their status quo." He proclaimed that his aim was to teach the Have-Nots "how to organize for power: how to get it and to use it."

Alinsky's second chapter, called "Of Means and Ends," craftily posed many difficult moral dilemmas, and established his "tenth rule of the ethics of means and ends," namely: "you do what you can with what you have and clothe it with moral arguments."

Alinsky didn't ignore traditional moral standards or dismiss them as unnecessary. He was much more devious than that. Instead, he taught his followers that "Moral rationalization is indispensable at all times of action whether to justify the selection or the use of ends or means." He reminded his trainees that "all effective actions require the passport of morality."

Alinsky certainly didn't mean that all actions must be moral. He meant that you decide what you want or need to do and then garb your actions in the language of morality. Phrase your goals, he enjoined his trainees, in "general terms like 'Liberty, Equality, Fraternity,' 'Of the Common Welfare,' 'Pursuit of Happiness,' or 'Bread and Peace.'" As Alinsky understood, the Communists also used words like "democracy" and "equality," but they had no relation whatsoever to what ordinary Americans understood by those terms.

At the same time, Alinsky admonished his organizers to see themselves as generals in a war, a war in which no rules of fair play exist and no compromise is permitted.

Recognizing the importance of words, Alinsky demanded that his organizers use the word "power," which he considered a word of force, vigor, and simplicity. Power was what he wanted—and he didn't have time for those who shrank from using this robust word. He advised his followers not "to pander to those who have no stomach for straight language."

In the chapter called "The Education of an Organizer," Alinsky explained that he conducted "a special training school for organizers with a full-time, fifteen-month program." It wasn't an easy regimen, Alinsky warned; it "requires frequent long conferences on organizational problems, analysis of power patterns, communication, conflict tactics, the education and development of community leaders, and the methods of introduction of new issues."

The qualities Alinsky looked for in a good organizer were ego ("reaching for the highest level for which man can reach—to create, to be a 'great creator,' to play God"); curiosity (raising "questions that agitate, that break through the accepted pattern"); irreverence ("nothing is sacred": the organizer "detests dogma, defies any finite definition of morality"); imagination ("the fuel for the force that keeps an organizer organizing"); a sense of humor ("the most potent weapons known to mankind are satire and ridicule"); and an organized personality with confidence in presenting the right reason for his actions only "as a moral rationalization after the right end has been achieved."

In the chapter on "Communication," Alinsky taught his organizers how to direct his people while letting them think they are making their own decisions. The organizer should develop skills in the manipulative technique of asking "loaded questions designed to elicit particular responses and to steer the organization's decision-making process in the direction which the organizer prefers."

The chapter called "In the Beginning" described how to train the community organizer in stealthy ways to make himself acceptable to the Have-Nots in the local community. "From the moment the organizer enters a community he lives, dreams, eats, breathes, sleeps only one thing and that is to build the mass power base of what he calls the army. Until he has developed that mass power base, he confronts no major issues."

The organizer's "biggest job is to give the people the feeling that they can do something." The organizer's job is "to build confidence and hope in the idea of organization and thus in the people themselves: to win limited victories, each of which will build confidence." The organizer will learn that "change comes from power, and power comes from organization."

"The organizer's first job is to create the issues or problems," and "organizations must be based on many issues." The organizer "must first rub raw the resentments of the people of the community; fan the latent hostilities of many of the people to the point of overt expression. He must search out controversy and issues, rather than avoid them, for unless there is controversy people are not concerned enough to act.... An organizer must stir up dissatisfaction and discontent."

The organizer "begins his 'trouble making' by stirring up these angers, frustrations, and resentments, and highlighting specific issues or grievances that heighten controversy." The organizer must remember that "organizations need action as an individual needs oxygen. The cessation of action brings death to the organization."

At the same time, he wrote, "The job of the organizer is to maneuver and bait the establishment so that it will publicly attack him as a 'dangerous enemy.'" Alinsky reminded his organizers that "to attempt to operate on a good-will rather than on a power basis would be to attempt something that the world has not yet experienced."

Alinsky's book is full of examples of issues and organizational victories from the decade of the 1960s (such as the Vietnam War, civil rights litigation, urban renewal, and campus riots), which are not meaningful to younger Americans today. They emphasize his strategy, however, that organizers must use current issues and "must be aware of the tremendous importance of understanding the part played by rationalization on a mass basis."

In the chapter called "Tactics," Alinsky told his trainees that power is not only what you have but what the enemy thinks you have: "The threat is usually more terrifying than the thing itself." He lists some of his recommended tactics:

- "Pick the target, freeze it, personalize it, and polarize it."
- "Keep the pressure on, with different tactics and actions."
- "The major premise for tactics is the development of operations that will maintain a constant pressure upon the opposition."
- "Multiple issues mean constant action and life" for the cause.
- "Ridicule is man's most potent weapon." Alinsky's advice was to "laugh at the enemy" to provoke "irrational anger."
- "A mass impression can be lasting and intimidating."
- "Make the enemy live up to their own book of rules."
- "You can club them to death with their 'book' of rules and regulations."
- A leader may struggle toward a decision and weigh the merits and demerits of an approach to a problem, but he must convince the people that "their cause is 100 percent on the side of the angels, and that the opposition are 100 percent on the side of the devil," even though that is a lie because there is "really only a 10 percent difference." To Alinsky, it is the necessity of transferring power that justifies this lie.

Alinsky described some of his successful mass demonstrations:

- Buying 100 tickets to a Rochester symphony concert for 100 blacks, and feeding them lots of baked beans beforehand so that they had to get up and go to the restroom during the first musical selection. This created "a combination not only of noise but also of odor, what you might call natural stink bombs." He reminded his readers that there is nothing illegal about needing to rush to the restroom.

- Tying up all the restrooms at Chicago's O'Hare Airport by having his demonstrators lock themselves in the toilet booths equipped with a book to read, and then staying there all day.
- Dropping wads of chewing gum all over the walks on a college campus.
- Paralyzing a bank by having 100 people show up at once with $5 or $10 to open a savings account (which they would then come back to close the following day). There is nothing illegal about this, but it created chaos for the bank. Alinsky called this "a middle-class guerrilla attack."
- Engaging in proxy fights with corporations.

Alinsky revealed his total contempt for the Haves and their devotion to self-interest: "I feel confident that I could persuade a millionaire on a Friday to subsidize a revolution for Saturday out of which he would make a huge profit on Sunday even though he was certain to be executed on Monday."

When Alinsky approached the end of his *Rules for Radicals* and projected future strategies in the chapter entitled "The Way Ahead," he laid out his plan to go after "America's white middle class. That is where the power is." They are the "Have-a-Little, Want Mores."

Alinsky boasted, "With rare exceptions, our activists and radicals are products of and rebels against our middle-class society.... Our rebels have contemptuously rejected the values and way of life of the middle class."

Here is where Alinsky's hypocrisy and duplicity became obvious. He had trained his community organizer to adopt a "middle-class identity" and familiarity with middle class "values and problems" in order to organize his "own people." Now, realizing "the priceless value of his middle-class experience," the organizer will "begin to dissect and examine that way of life as he never has before." "Everything now has a different meaning and purpose."

Alinsky instructed his trainees to "return to the suburban scene of your middle class with its variety of organizations from PTAs to League of Women Voters, consumer groups, churches, and clubs. The job is to search out the leaders in these various activities, identify their major issues, find areas of common agreement, and excite their imagination with tactics that can introduce drama and adventure into the tedium of middle class life."

Alinsky cautioned his organizers: "Start them easy, don't scare them off." When Alinsky's community organizer moves from organizing the "poor" to organizing the "middle class," he "discards the rhetoric that always says 'pig.' . . . He will view with strategic sensitivity the nature of middle-class behavior with its hangups over rudeness or aggressive, insulting, profane actions. All this and more must be grasped and used to radicalize parts of the middle class."

These are the strategies that helped nominate and elect Barack Obama president of the United States. They were also deployed to push through his radical legislation, gigantic spending programs, government-imposed secularism, and squashing of religious freedom.

The *New York Times* laid out this Alinksyite plan on its January 26, 2009, front page, under the headline "Retooling a Grass-Roots Network to Serve a YouTube Presidency." Obama's staff, it reported, has already started "transforming the YouTubing-Facebooking-texting-Twittering grass-roots organization that put Mr. Obama in the White House into an instrument of government. That is something that Mr. Obama, who began his career as a community organizer, told aides was a top priority, even before he was elected."

President Obama's staff created a group, headquartered in the offices of the Democratic National Committee, called "Organizing for America." Its mission: to "redirect the campaign machinery into the service of broad changes in health care, environmental and fiscal policy. They envision an army of supporters talking, sending e-mail messages and texting to friends and neighbors as they try to mold public opinion." Three days after Obama was sworn in as president, an announcement video was sent to 13 million people.

Obama's team understood that traditional methods of communicating with voters would be superseded by new media built around social networking. In the 2008 campaign, liberals dominated fundraising on the internet, with Obama outraising McCain there by more than ten to one. The Obama campaign exploited this advantage fully and profitably, not just in raising money but in unleashing liberal bloggers, who were especially active in savaging Sarah Palin.

This twenty-first-century use of internet technology and new-media communication accounted for Obama's astonishing record of money-raising. He raised nearly $750 million for his presidential campaign. By contrast, in 2004, George W. Bush and Senator John Kerry together collected less than $650 million. For the general election, Obama had more than three times what John McCain had at his disposal, and Obama still had $30 million in the bank after the election.

Obama's technology/internet superiority continued into his first term. In 2009, DailyKos.com, a liberal blog site, ranked 3,631 in daily traffic out of many millions of internet websites. This is far higher, often by a factor of 100, than conservative sites. Many other liberal websites also outrank conservative sites, such as MoveOn.org, a website started a decade ago to defend Bill Clinton during his myriad scandals.

Previous presidents recorded and released a radio speech every Saturday morning, but Obama instead records a video speech, then posts it on the White House website and YouTube where it can be picked up and forwarded to millions of followers who weren't listening to radio on Saturday mornings. His first speech was a pitch for his $825 billion economic so-called Stimulus package. By Sunday afternoon, more than 600,000 people had viewed it on YouTube. He would later make similar use of internet technology to put a gloss on his HHS mandate and his "evolving" endorsement of gay marriage.

STILL ON THE PROWL

Alinsky's devils still prowl about the country, seeking the ruin of "Haves." Barack Obama is the consummation of Alinsky's plan. Obama, following Alinsky's advice about the manipulation of the middle class, dutifully calls himself the "Middle Class President." And, as Alinsky taught, Obama always clothes his arguments for immorality in moral garb. Whether the issue is abortion or gay marriage, Obama always claims the moral high ground.

One of Obama's favorite props for Alinskyite propaganda is his own children. By connecting his policies to his children, he hopes to make those policies look less radical. During the 2008 campaign, he cited his children in answer to a question from a voter about his support for sexual education in public schools:

> When it comes specifically to HIV/AIDS, the most important prevention is education, which should include—which should include abstinence education and teaching the children—teaching children, you know, that sex is not something casual. But it should also include—it should also include other, you know, information about contraception because, look, I've got two daughters, 9 years old and 6 years old. I am going to teach them first of all about values and morals. But if they make a mistake, I don't want them punished with a baby. I don't want

them punished with an STD at the age of 16. You know, so it doesn't make sense to not give them information.

He didn't want his daughters "punished with a baby." In 2012, during the flap over Georgetown student Sandra Fluke's right-to-contraception crusade, Obama cited his daughters again.

Rush Limbaugh had likened Fluke to a "prostitute" for demanding that priests and nuns at Georgetown finance her fornication. Limbaugh later apologized to Fluke; despite Limbaugh's apology, President Obama blasted him, saying that he would be happy to see his daughters imitate Fluke without harassment from the likes of Rush. Obama had called up Fluke to commiserate with her, explaining to the press: "The reason I called Ms. Fluke is because I thought about Malia and Sasha, and one of the things I want them to do as they get older is to engage in issues they care about, even ones I may not agree with them on. I want them to be able to speak their mind in a civil and thoughtful way. And I don't want them attacked or called horrible names because they're being good citizens."

His daughters proved useful to him again when he was asked his reason for embracing gay marriage. It was a product of "personal reflection," he said, stimulated by conversations with his daughters, who attend the posh and gay-friendly school Sidwell Friends with adopted children of LGBT couples.

"Malia and Sasha, they have friends whose parents are same-sex couples. There have been times where Michelle and I have been sitting around the dinner table and we're talking about their friends and their parents," said Obama. "[For] Malia and Sasha, it wouldn't dawn on them that somehow their friends' parents would be treated differently. It doesn't make sense to them and frankly, that's the kind of thing that prompts a change in perspective."

Even Saul Alinsky, were he still alive today, might have chuckled at that skillfully deployed whopper.

CHAPTER SIX

USEFUL IDIOTS

Throughout his career, Obama has been supported by the Christian left, whose leaders give him moral cover for an otherwise secularist agenda. Indeed, subverting Christian churches has been a long-standing strategy of the left to gain the moral high ground for their "progressive" causes.

George Soros, for instance, has subsidized Protestant front groups that helped elect Obama in 2008 and that are now working furiously for his reelection. The magazine *Sojourners*, led by Jim Wallis, stands out as the flagship publication for Obama's longstanding dupe-the-Protestants operation. Soros has been shoveling cash to the organization that funds the magazine (which is also called Sojourners).

"George Soros, one of the leading billionaire leftists—he has financed groups promoting abortion, atheism, same-sex marriage, and gargantuan government—bankrolled Sojourners with a $200,000 grant in 2004," wrote Marvin Olasky, the editor of *World*, an evangelical magazine, in 2010. "Since then Sojourners has received at least two more grants from Soros organizations. Sojourners revenues have more than tripled—from $1,601,171 in 2001–2002 to $5,283,650 in 2008–2009—as secular leftists have learned to use the religious left to elect Obama and others."

The reelection efforts of the pro-Obama Protestant left and the pro-Obama Catholic left often overlap. Money from Soros, in fact, has flowed through Jim Wallis to former staff members of Catholics in Alliance for the Common Good. A Wallis-led group called Faith in Public Life—which was set up to help elect Obama in 2008—scooped up several former staffers from Catholics in Alliance for the Common Good. A former assistant media director for the United States Conference of Catholic bishops, John Gehring, has been a senior writer for Faith in Public Life and has written for "God's Politics," a blog run by Wallis.

Wallis's self-described "ecumenical" undertaking is Alinskyite to the core. In recent years, Wallis has gone to great lengths to present himself as a moderate in the hopes of fooling evangelicals into voting for Obama's reelection. But his resume is one of hard leftism and repeated praise of Communists in Central America and Asia (he called the Communist conquest of South Vietnam an exhilarating moment in his life).

"Wallis, who was the president of the radical Students for a Democratic Society (SDS) during his college days and is a stout supporter of Alinskyian faith-based organizing, is certainly aware of the organizing adage: 'You do what you can with what you have and clothe it with moral garments…all effective action requires the passport of morality,'" according to writer Stephanie Block, who covered the creation of Faith in Public Life.

Wallis founded Faith in Public Life to be a gathering spot and organizing network for Alinskyite Protestants and Catholics who were eager to see Obama elected in 2008. Block reported that affiliates of Wallis's group included chapters of Catholic Charities, Catholic Relief Services, Catholic Social Services, Call to Action, Pax Christi, Dignity, a smattering of liberal Protestant and Jewish groups, as well as secularists determined to harness the power of religion for their own purposes. The Ford Foundation, Barbra Streisand, and the Rockefellers have donated to Wallis's foundation over the years.

Many of the organizations attached to Faith in Public Life have Alinskyite ties. "Among Faith in Public Life affiliates are hundreds of faith-based groups and their member institutions, from all around the country, and all of them related to the organizational theories of Saul Alinsky. Most of them fall into their own networks...producing a dizzying array of names and acronyms, but besides history, they have structural and 'prophetic' commonalities," reported Block.

In 2011, the Democratic National Committee (DNC) hired an evangelical pastor, the Reverend Derrick Harkins, who is affiliated with Faith in Public Life, to head up its "faith outreach" efforts—the equivalent of the Republican National Committee hiring a conservative Catholic bishop to drum up votes for Mitt Romney.

"DC Pastor to Woo Votes for Obama," reported the *Washington Post* in October 2011. "Harkins is the first member of the faith outreach staff that the party has announced for the 2012 election. In 2008, the campaign made strides in attracting religious voters long considered GOP property, particularly white evangelicals. Recent polls show weakened support for Obama among such groups, and some experts on faith outreach say Harkins's work with progressive and conservative evangelicals in particular could help."

Harkins, continued the story, "leads Nineteenth Street Baptist Church in Northwest Washington, a predominantly African American congregation known for elite as well as solidly middle-class members."

Terry Lynch explained the DNC's tapping of Harkins as Chicago-style politics, telling the *Post*:

> "I think they realize the excitement isn't there from the first campaign, which was like a revival," said Terry Lynch, executive director of the Downtown Cluster of Congregations and a longtime activist in faith and politics in the District. "They need help with their base, and Harkins is a bellwether."

The *Post* continued:

> "Harkins brings the assets of Obama's Chicago church but without the baggage," Lynch said, a reference to the president's former place of worship, Trinity United Church of Christ, where Obama was close to the Rev. Jeremiah Wright, the controversial pastor.

The *Post* noted that "Obama in 2008 picked up five percentage points of support among white evangelicals over John F. Kerry in 2004 (26 percent vs. 21 percent) and nearly three times the percentage of those younger than 40 (33 percent vs. 12 percent)," but that he had lost his touch with the religious during the Democrats' shellacking in congressional elections in 2010. Harkins was hired to stop this bleeding.

The *Post* ran another story about Harkins after Obama's endorsement of gay marriage—"An Evangelical in Obama's Corner." Harkins was now busy having to convince black pastors that support for gay marriage sprung from the president's "values" and "faith." Harkins "bristled," according to the paper, when asked if the religious might think twice before reelecting a president who supports abortion and gay marriage. The Democratic Party, said Harkins, "doesn't revolve around one or two hot-button issues."

THE UNHOLY ALLIANCE

No, the Democratic Party has come to revolve around a whole galaxy of secular and socialist-leaning issues, all of which empower the state, which makes it all the more ironic that there is even such a thing as a "Catholic left," because the Catholic Church has always opposed statism and secularism. But in the United States, the effort to subvert the Church goes back decades, is traceable to Saul Alinksy, and among its direct beneficiaries was Barack Obama, when he was a community organizer in Chicago.

Thomas Pauken, in his book *The Thirty Years War*, noted that:

> Over the years, many young nuns and priests had fallen under the spell of Saul Alinsky, who based his community organizing operation in Chicago. Alinsky had decided early on in his career that he had to change the attitudes of the Catholic Church in the United States which traditionally had been viewed as a conservative, anti-Communist religious institution. His objective was to use his young "recruits" from the religious ranks as a wedge inside the institution of the church in order to change it. As the Alinsky-trained recruits grew older and gained more power within the Church infrastructure, the Catholic Church in America began to show the effects.
>
> The radicalization of elements of the Catholic clergy turned out to be one of Saul Alinsky's most significant accomplishments. His decades of hard work paid off as the religious who shared Alinsky's radical brand of politics moved into key positions of influence within the bureaucracy of various religious orders, Catholic dioceses, and even the United States Catholic Conference itself.

In the 1980s, the Catholic archdiocese of Chicago contributed to the training of Obama in the very Alinskyite radicalism that would culminate in such anti-religious measures as the HHS mandate. In fact, in the course of writing this book, we met a source who once had access to copies of documents from the archives of the Chicago archdiocese. This source supplied us with never-before-published copies of invoices, checks, and letters that confirm the Church's support for the man who would one day seek to destroy its religious freedom.

In a series of appendices, we have reproduced the check and invoice showing that the archdiocese of Chicago paid for Obama's plane trip to a conference in Los Angeles run by the Industrial Areas Foundation, the community organizing group founded by Alinsky.

Alinsky had always targeted churches for radical infiltration, and to a certain degree he succeeded. The Catholic Campaign for Human Development (CCHD) was the Alinskyite branch of the United States Conference of Catholic Bishops which had offices in dioceses across the country. It was founded in 1969 by priests and bishops close to Saul Alinsky, such as Monsignor John Egan, who sat on Alinsky's Industrial Areas Foundation board. The group was originally called the Campaign for Human Development, with "Catholic" added later as its socialist work began to draw criticism.

Alinsky had initially won favor with some in the Archdiocese of Chicago by appearing to be an advocate of justice for the poor. In the 1950s, in fact, Alinsky received tens of thousands of dollars from the Church to "study" poverty and racism. As the *Chicago Tribune* reported in a remembrance of Alinsky in 1985:

> Samuel Cardinal Stritch, at the time the head of Chicago's Catholic archdiocese, then hired Alinsky to draw up a scheme to preserve the city's older neighborhoods from the urban-renewal bulldozers and at the same time help in the peaceful integration of Chicago's growing black and Hispanic populations.

Alinsky sent out three organizer-researcher apprentices to do the leg work: Nicholas von Hoffman and Lester Hunt, who had been trying to organize Puerto Ricans on the South Side when Alinsky discovered them, and Father [later made a monsignor] John J. Egan, a young, socially aware Catholic priest with good Chicago connections.

Alinsky never made any bones about his reason for partnering with the Church: he needed her organizing power. "Well, the first thing I did, the first thing I always do, is to move into the community as an observer, to talk with people and listen and learn their grievances and their attitudes. Then I look around at what I've got to work with, what levers I can use to pry closed doors open, what institutions or organizations already exist that can be useful," he said. "In the case of Back of the Yards, the area was 95 percent Roman Catholic, and I recognized that if I could win the support of the Church, we'd be off and running. Conversely, without the Church, or at least some elements of it, it was unlikely that we'd be able to make much of a dent in the community."

In the mid-1980s, Obama was employed by Jerry Kellman of the Calumet Community Religious Conference. Obama was a community organizer of one of its offshoots, the Developing Communities Project, which received grant support from the Catholic Campaign for Human Development. The Developing Communities Project was not an official part of the Church, though Bishop Norbert Felix Gaughan of Gary, Indiana (a diocese that adjoins Chicago) acted as if it was and drafted a letter to bully pastors into supporting Kellman's and Obama's socialist organizing. (The draft of the letter is reproduced in the appendices.)

According to Obama biographer David Remnick, Chicago Cardinal Joseph Bernardin went so far as to say that priests who refused to work with Kellman and Obama were committing grave sin. "Kellman's early attempt to organize church leaders in the area got a boost when Cardinal

Joseph Bernardin signaled that if local priests didn't join the effort they should rush to confession," writes Remnick.

In enjoying the patronage of left-leaning liberals inside the Catholic Church, Kellman and Obama were imitating their hero. Alinsky started the Industrial Areas Foundation with the help of an auxiliary bishop of Chicago, Bernard J. Sheil, who introduced Alinsky to his champagne socialist friends in Chicago and New York City from whom Alinsky would later raise money. As Alinsky harnessed the power of Catholic churches in Chicago for socialist organizing, so did Kellman and Obama; in fact, Obama started his career as a community organizer in the rectory rooms of a South Side Chicago parish.

"Barack Obama was in the Main Reading Room of the New York Public Library on Forty-second Street, leafing through newspapers, searching for the work he wanted most," reports David Remnick.

> He picked up a copy of *Community Jobs*, a small paper that carried ads for public service work. In Chicago, an organizer named Jerry Kellman, a follower (more or less) of the Alinsky tradition, was looking for someone to work with him on the South Side where the steel mills were closing and thousands of people were facing unemployment and a blistered landscape of deteriorating housing, toxic-waste dumps, bad schools, gangs, drugs, and violent crime. Kellman, who led the Calumet Community Religious Conference, a coalition of churches designed to help the people in the area, was especially desperate for an African-American organizer. The neighborhoods on the far South Side were nearly all black and he, as a wiry-haired white Jewish guy from New York, needed help.

Obama looked at the "long and descriptive" ad, writes Remnick, who talked to Kellman for his book. "'I figured if I could paint a picture of the devastation and show it as a multiracial but mainly black area, it would interest someone,' Kellman said. The address at the bottom of the ad was 351 East 113th Street, Father Bill Stenzel's rectory at Holy Rosary, a Catholic church on the far South Side. Kellman was using a couple of rooms there as his base of operations."

Obama got this job in 1983. Curiously, in *Dreams from My Father*, Obama creates a composite character named "Marty Kaufman." But Chicago journalists had no problem identifying "Marty Kaufman" as Jerry Kellman. In his memoir, Obama relates that as "Marty" drove him around Chicago, he told him about the cynical origins of the Calumet Community Religious Conference's manipulation of the Church:

> As we reentered the highway, Marty began to tell me more about the organization he built. The idea had first come to him two years earlier, he said, when he'd read reports of the plant closings and layoffs, then sweeping across South Chicago and the southern suburbs. With the help of a sympathetic Catholic auxiliary bishop, he'd gone to meet with pastors and church members in the area, and heard both blacks and whites talk about their shame of unemployment, their fear of losing a house, of being cheated out of a pension—their common sense of having been betrayed.
>
> "Most of our work is with churches," he said. "If poor and working-class people want to build real power, they have to have some sort of institutional base. With the unions in the shape they're in, the churches are the only game in town. That's where the people are, and that's where the values are, even if they've been buried under a lot of bullshit. Churches won't work with you, though, just out of the goodness of their hearts. They'll talk a good game—a sermon on Sunday, maybe, or a special offering for the homeless. But if push

comes to shove, they won't really move unless you can show them how it'll help them pay their heating bill."

Matt Vadum, a senior editor at the Capital Research Center in Washington, D.C., has studied Obama's exploitative partnership with the Catholic Church in Chicago. Vadum has also studied the checkered Catholic Campaign for Human Development, which still distributes grants to groups headed up by Alinskyite community organizers. In an interview for this book, Vadum described Obama's relationship with the Catholic Church as an audacious and opportunistic exercise in parasitism. "Barack Obama seems ambivalent about the Roman Catholic Church. When it was to his advantage he used the Church to advance his career but when the Church, with its steadfast opposition to artificial birth control, became an obstacle to his grand plan to remake America he promptly turned against it."

In Vadum's view, "Obama understands that angry people open to the gospel of envy and so-called social justice are easy to find in churches. Once identified, they can be recruited and used to help inject the poison of socialism into the American body politic." Vadum notes that the "vibrant leftist community within the Catholic Church makes it an ideal breeding ground for radical activists. Catholics were helpful to Obama when he was cutting his teeth as a leftist agitator."

Vadum, too, sees the bitter irony of Obama launching his political career (of which community organizing was the opening part) from a rectory office at Holy Rosary Church in Chicago. Vadum quoted back to me Obama's own words: "Obama has said, 'I got my start as a community organizer working with mostly Catholic parishes on the South Side of Chicago that were struggling because the steel plants had closed.'" He quoted Obama again, who had said, "very early on, my career was intertwined with the belief in social justice that is so strong in the Church." Vadum told me that "like the atheist Saul Alinsky before him, who relied heavily on his fellow traveler friends in the Catholic priesthood, Obama found Catholics convenient."

Rey Flores, the former Chicago director of the Catholic Campaign for Human Development, has also studied the crass political alliance between Obama and the Catholic left. Flores, who left CCHD in 2010 disgusted by its subversion of Catholic orthodoxy, is now the Executive Director of Better Catholic Giving, which presents itself as the antithesis of CCHD in that it seeks "to advocate for effective poverty-relief initiatives that are one-hundred percent in line with the teachings of the Catholic Church." On his website, Flores explains how the CCHD has long operated as a de facto arm of the Democratic Party and the progressive movement. By the time Obama arrived on the scene, he writes, CCHD had reached a high point of radicalism:

> [It] became a *pigs trough* for the left-leaning community organizing activities that Chicago is so well-known for. Back before his demise in 1972, it wasn't so much that Saul Alinsky sought to latch on to Chicago's Catholic clergy and their seemingly endless collection basket dollars, it was really the bishops themselves who rolled the red carpet out to Alinsky, mainly Monsignor Jack Egan who was apparently enthralled with Alinsky's rabble-rousing ways.

Flores's disenchantment with CCHD grew over the years as its contempt for official Church teaching and lack of interest in any kingdom beyond this world became clear to him. In an article for the online magazine *Crisis* in November 2011, he wrote: "While I was the Director of the Chicago CCHD, I was told by some of the left-leaning clergy that we should not be talking about spiritual poverty in regard to the CCHD's goals. If a group claims that the Catholic Church is no longer interested in helping save the souls of the poor, then something inside that group is certainly rotten."

Indeed, from 1998–2008, CCHD gave $7.3 million of Catholic-donated money to the now notorious ACORN, the Association of Community Organizations for Reform Now, a radical leftist organization that supported Barack Obama's brand of "community organizing." In 2007 alone, CCHD increased its support of ACORN, giving ACORN thirty-seven grants totaling $1,037,000. During 2007–2008, ACORN and its affiliated organizations were aggressively registering what they claimed were 1.3 million poor people to vote. ACORN focused on new registrations in the key toss-up states of Ohio, Michigan, Pennsylvania, and Florida.

CCHD knew exactly how ACORN spent its money. CCHD's executive director, Ralph McCloud, admitted to Catholic News Service that "some of the funds that the Catholic Campaign contributed to ACORN in the past undoubtedly were used for voter registration drives."

Even though the pro-Obama political activity of ACORN had been widely reported, and even though employees of ACORN and affiliated organizations like Project Vote had either been indicted or convicted of submitting false voter registration forms in fourteen states, CCHD, in June 2008, approved grants of $1.13 million to forty local ACORN affiliates for the cycle beginning July 1, 2008. Those grants were ratified by the United States Conference of Catholic Bishops at its June 2008 meeting.

Under press scrutiny and backlash from members of the laity, the CCHD-ACORN relationship suddenly became too embarrassing for the bishops to ignore, and CCHD announced it was suspending (not canceling) the 2008 grants. Revealingly, the reason given for suspension was not ACORN's partisan political activity or registration frauds; it was because Dale Rathke, the brother of ACORN founder Wade Rathke, had embezzled nearly $1 million from the organization and its affiliates back in 1999 and 2000.

In the light of this history, it is no coincidence that Obama won 54 percent of the Catholic vote in 2008. His Chicago-style Alinskyite strategy worked where the Catholic John Kerry's secularist strategy, which lost the Catholic vote to George W. Bush 47 percent to 52 percent, had failed.

OBAMA AT NOTRE DAME

Nor is it any surprise that in his first year of office the U.S. bishops' most prestigious university, Notre Dame, invited Obama to speak at the school's graduation ceremonies and conferred upon him an honorary law degree.

When Obama was a community organizer, Cardinal Bernardin had singled him out for special praise. In his typical style of self-referential speechmaking, Obama returned the praise, telling Notre Dame's graduating seniors:

> I found myself drawn—not just to work with the church, but to be in the church. It was through this service that I was brought to Christ. At the time, Cardinal Joseph Bernardin was the archbishop of Chicago. For those of you too young to have known him, he was a kind and good and wise man. A saintly man. I can still remember him speaking at one of the first organizing meetings I attended on the South Side. He stood as both a lighthouse and a crossroads—unafraid to speak his mind on moral issues ranging from poverty, AIDS, and abortion to the death penalty and nuclear war. And yet, he was congenial and gentle in his persuasion, always trying to bring people together; always trying to find common ground. Just before he died, a reporter asked Cardinal Bernardin about this approach to his ministry. And he said,

"You can't really get on with preaching the Gospel until you've touched minds and hearts."

...But as you leave here today, remember the lessons of Cardinal Bernardin, of Father Hesburgh, of movements for change both large and small. Remember that each of us, endowed with the dignity possessed by all children of God, has the grace to recognize ourselves in one another; to understand that we all seek the same love of family and the same fulfillment of a life well lived. Remember that in the end, we are all fishermen.

Even so, Obama told Notre Dame's graduates that they should view the official doctrines of the Catholic Church as too doubtful for any real use in public life:

Hold firm to your faith and allow it to guide you on your journey. Stand as a lighthouse. But remember too that the ultimate irony of faith is that it necessarily admits doubt. It is the belief in things not seen. It is beyond our capacity as human beings to know with certainty what God has planned for us or what he asks of us, and those of us who believe must trust that his wisdom is greater than our own.

This doubt should not push us away from our faith. But it should humble us. It should temper our passions, and cause us to be wary of self-righteousness. It should compel us to remain open, and curious, and eager to continue the moral and spiritual debate that began for so many of you within the walls of Notre Dame. And within our vast democracy, this doubt should remind us to persuade through reason, through an appeal whenever we can to universal rather than parochial principles, and most of all through an abiding example of

good works, charity, kindness, and service that moves hearts
and minds.

So once again—contrary to traditional Catholic thinking—faith and
reason are separate. Reason is liberalism. Faith should be subordinate to
it. That is the Obama catechism, and it should have been a scandal that
a Catholic university invited him to deliver this alternative catechism to
its graduating seniors.

As Obama geared up to pass laws that would violate fundamental
moral teachings of the Church and cripple her institutions, a university
named after Jesus Christ's mother handed him an honorary law degree
that championed him as a community organizer for the world. The
degree read in part:

> A community organizer who honed his advocacy for the poor,
> the marginalized and the worker in the streets of Chicago, he
> now organizes a larger community, bringing to the world a
> renewed American dedication to diplomacy and dialogue
> with all nations and religions committed to human rights and
> the global common good.

Tellingly, while some bishops objected to Obama's honorary degree
from Notre Dame, others remained silent, and some of Cardinal Bernardin's protégés praised the decision. Archbishop Michael J. Sheehan of
Santa Fe, New Mexico, said that he supported Notre Dame's decision to
confer an honorary degree upon Barack Obama and could not understand the "big scene" of protests about it. Asked by the *National Catholic
Reporter* if other bishops agreed with him, he replied, "Of course, the
majority." He declared that "we don't want to isolate ourselves from the
rest of America by our strong views on abortion and the other things."
Though normally sensitive to the etiquette of ecumenism, he then

allowed himself a slight at the expense of another religious group: "We'd be like the Amish, you know, kind of isolated from society, if we kept pulling back because of a single issue."

Sheehan explained his position by pointing to his experience with Bernardin. "I believe in collaboration," Sheehan said. "I worked under Cardinal Bernardin and he taught me how to collaborate, how to consult. So I am very committed to the concept called shared responsibility. I think involving people in the process all the way along—my priests, my lay people, I am open to talking to them, working with them. Consultation, collaboration, building bridges not burning them." That sounds very nice until one realizes that collaboration with supporters of morally evil policies—such as partial-birth abortion—is not exactly what the Church teaches.

Notre Dame wasn't the only Catholic school eager to honor Obama. The faculty at Jesuit Georgetown University in Washington, D.C., had already honored him with their campaign donations. Professors and priests there dumped $178,000 into his campaign coffers. The *Chronicle of Higher Education* ranked Georgetown's faculty among the top ten academic donors to Obama.

Some priests and nuns had even worked on his campaign. Obama quickly cobbled together a "Catholic advisory committee" that included such longtime leftist nuns as Sister Jamie Phelps, O.P., Professor of Theology at Xavier University, and Sister Catherine Pinkerton with the Congregation of St. Joseph.

Even the Vatican, after his election, wanted to give Obama the benefit of the doubt. On April 29, 2009, Vatican City's official newspaper, *L'Osservatore Romano*, ran a highly sympathetic front-page article by Giuseppe Fiorentino, a liberal writer on foreign affairs, about Barack Obama's record. The article claimed that Obama had "moved with caution," and that fears about his pro-abortion record were unfounded, as he "does not seem to have established the radical changes that he had

aired" and might even be "rebalancing" his policies "in support of moth-
erhood." Giovanni Maria Vian, editor of *L'Osservatore Romano*, was
similarly gulled, saying in 2009, "Obama is not a pro-abortion president."
And former papal household theologian Cardinal Georges Cottier con-
gratulated Obama for his "humble realism." *Washington Post* columnist
E. J. Dionne, who uses his "Catholicism" to advance Obama's cause in
the mainstream media, enjoys seeing traditional Catholics in America
get their wires crossed with ostensible allies at the U.S. Conference of
Catholic Bishops and the Vatican. The "Vatican clearly views Obama
through a broader prism," sniffed Dionne after the remarks of Vian and
Cottier.

The Vatican would soon realize that it had misjudged the president.
Indeed, if one were to give Obama a political rating according to the
official moral teachings of the Church, it would be zero. On every single
contested issue that touches on the natural moral law—from abortion
to gay marriage to euthanasia to dispensing abortifacients to teens—
Obama stands against the moral teachings of the Church. And yet, so
clever is his appeal, and so active is the Catholic left, that Obama could
still win the Catholic vote. Liberal "Catholic" newspapers and maga-
zines—such as the *National Catholic Reporter*, the Jesuit publication
America, and *Commonweal*, all of which have editorialized in support
of Obama's HHS mandate—still appear on coffee tables in the foyers of
chanceries. In May 2012, Jesuit Georgetown honored Kathleen Sebelius,
one of the architects of the mandate, at a commencement ceremony for
its Public Policy Institute.

And those who helped fool Catholic voters in 2008 are back again in
2012. Alexia Kelley, who was co-founder and director of the pro-Obama
Catholics in Alliance for the Common Good, now directs the federal
Health and Human Services Department's Center for Faith-Based and
Community Initiatives. Instead of closing down George W. Bush's
"faith-based" offices, as many people expected he would do, Obama has

kept them open and used the "religious" as lobbyists for his legislation. Kelley is a product of the Alinskyite infiltration of the Church. For almost a decade, Kelley worked for the U.S. Conference of Catholic Bishops on the Catholic Campaign for Human Development. During the years that Kelley worked for CCHD, more than seven million dollars were awarded to ACORN, reported Anne Hendershott in *Catholic World Report* in 2011.

Kelley paired up with Catholics United's leaders, James Salt and Chris Korzen, in the 2008 campaign for Obama. Salt's previous political work included orchestrating the Kansas Democratic Party's sham "faith outreach" efforts, according to Hendershott, who noted that this involved "messaging work" for Kathleen Sebelius.

Catholics United presents itself as "a non-profit, non-partisan organization dedicated to promoting the message of justice and the common good found at the heart of the Catholic Social Tradition," according to the group's literature. In reality, reported Hendershott, it is an arm of the Obama administration. In a September 12, 2008, radio interview, Korzen hinted at this function, revealing that at Catholics United "we do a little bit more edgy work...we can do lobbying and political work unlike your traditional non-profits."

In 2004, according to Hendershott, Korzen had served as co-founder and director of the Catholic front group for John Kerry, the Catholic Voting Project. Previous to that work, Korzen had logged time as an organizer with the Service Employees International Union. Korzen has also been a contributor to *The Huffington Post*, where he churned out quasi-religious propaganda for the Democratic Party in 2008—columns with such titles as "John McCain: Just How Pro-Life?" and "McCain Embraces Pastor Who Calls Catholicism a Cult." When Kathleen Sebelius ran into trouble with Catholics during her nomination hearings, Korzen was there to put out the fire, scooping up signatures for an online petition called "Catholics for Sebelius."

These "Catholic" front groups for Obama still exist and will play a role in his drive for reelection. Catholics in Alliance for the Common Good numbers among its donors some of the biggest names in progressive politics. George Soros was one of its first donors, giving it $50,000 in 2005 and then $100,000 the following year via his Open Society Institute.

These front groups enjoy ties to the U.S. Conference of Catholic Bishops, in which operatives sympathetic to the Democrats are still nested. Until recently, one of the USCCB's chief political advisers was a former White House aide under President Jimmy Carter, John Carr. Carr organized the White House Conference of Families as its executive director during Carter's one term. We went back and looked at the promotional literature for that Carr-directed event: it openly touted support for "abortion" and the use of the federal government's power to promote "family planning," not to mention "homosexual rights." Carr insists that he was always pro-life, but the promotion of such an anti-Catholic conference hardly constitutes sound preparation for a high-level job with the Catholic Church.

"John Carr has certainly been a major influence" on the USCCB, said writer Stephanie Block in an interview for this book. She notes that Carr, while working for the U.S. bishops, chaired the board of the Center for Community Change, a "progressive" group with ties to the pro-abortion community.

In May 2012, the Obama reelection campaign announced that it had hired a new "faith vote coordinator," Michael Wear. According to CNN, Wear was plucked from the White House Office of Faith-Based and Neighborhood Partnerships to join the campaign and put out fires related to the HHS-mandate backlash. "'I don't think the campaign originally had this position in its box,' said a source close to the campaign, who refused to speak on the record because the person was discussing sensitive issues," reported CNN. CNN also reported that Wear is a fallen-away Catholic.

SISTER OBAMACARE

Finally, aside from these Obama functionaries, there will be priests in collars and nuns (likely without habits) who will attempt to mislead Catholic voters about the policies of the Obama administration. Among the most shocking of these is Sister Carol Keehan, who has pursued an extraordinarily lucrative career as the head of the Catholic Health Association. A de facto lobbyist for Obama's agenda, Sister Keehan helped the president pass his health care bill in 2010 and then more recently helped him hammer out a "revision" to the HHS mandate in the hopes of hoodwinking gullible Catholics into voting for his reelection.

How much is Sister Keehan worth for such political interventions? We called up the Catholic Health Association to nail down her exact salary and benefits as the head of that pro-Obama group. We received some astonishing information. In 2010, Keehan, who belongs to the Daughters of Charity, pulled down $962,467 in salary and benefits, according to the group's Schedule J (Form 990). (The group is required by law to show this form to the public upon request.)

Why would a nun be earning nearly a million dollars a year in salary and benefits as the head of a group ostensibly concerned with the corporal works of mercy? The answer is alarming: the Catholic hospitals Keehan represents as chief executive officer of the Catholic Health Association (CHA) stand to receive hundreds of millions of dollars from the federal government if Obamacare holds up past 2012. While Catholic hospitals that uphold Catholic teaching could be forced to close, Catholic hospitals willing to comply with Obamacare's mandates could be richly rewarded. For this reason, executives at hospitals belonging to the association are more than happy to pay a huge salary and benefits to an executive skilled at manipulating the Catholic electorate for Obama. To them, Sister Keehan is worth every dime of her near-million-dollar compensation package. (Her 2011 salary/benefits, if past increases are any indication, should exceed a million dollars a year. Her 2010 salary/benefits jumped up over $100,000 from her 2009 figures.)

Theoretically, this queenly sum is paid to the nun's order, though CHA added a curious caveat to its compensation figures on the Schedule J:

> The descriptions below provide an overview of the composition of the five compensation figure columns (B, C, D, E and F). Note that for Sisters Carol Keehan and Patricia Talone and for Father Tom Nairn, all amounts in column B, except for certain fringe benefits included in column (B)(iii), were paid to their respective orders.

In other words, the religious orders don't receive all of the money. What are these "certain fringe benefits" to which the caveat refers? CHA provided no coherent answer to that question.

According to the form, base compensation for "Daughters of Charity for Sr. Keehan" was $682,982. "Bonus and incentive compensation" was $136,000. "Other reportable compensation"—which is the (B)(iii) to which the caveat refers—was $131,888. Nontaxable benefits were $11,597. All this adds up to salary and benefits totaling $962,467.

Left-wing "Catholic Social Justice" appears to be a good career move. Sister Talone, one of the other CHA executives to which the caveat refers above, generated for her order, the Sisters of Mercy, $416,623 in total compensation, while Fr. Nairn's order, the Franciscan Friars, got a chunk of his $194,947 in salary and benefits.

Obamacare will guarantee Catholic hospitals—or at least the ones that comply with the HHS mandate—another avalanche of federal government cash. "For where your treasure is, there your heart will be also," said Jesus Christ. A pedestrian reduction of this saying is: Follow the money. Sister Carol Keehan and company, for all their pious talk about "social justice," have a compelling financial incentive in seeing Obama reelected.

But amidst this scandalous support for Obama shines a ray of hope. Though the doggedly secularist dominant media almost entirely ignored this story, the bishops announced in May 2012 the filing of a historic lawsuit against the Obama administration by forty-three Catholic institutions, a group which included a representative slice of dioceses, schools, and apostolates across the country. Obama-honoring Notre Dame was even numbered among these entities suing him for his unconstitutional HHS fiat.

"We have tried negotiation with the Administration and legislation with Congress—and we'll keep at it—but there's still no fix. Time is running out," explained Cardinal Timothy Dolan, president of the U.S. Conference of Catholic Bishops. "Our valuable ministries and fundamental rights hang in the balance, so we have to resort to the courts now."

The suits describe the HHS mandate as a dagger aimed at the religious heart of historic America and contain a warning for all who will vote in November: "If the government can force religious institutions to violate their beliefs in such a manner, there is no apparent limit to the government's power."

CHAPTER SEVEN

ISLAM, THE
ONE EXCEPTION
TO OBAMA'S
SECULARISM

O bama, as chronicled in this book, is at war with Christianity, seeking to defeat it from without through regulatory decrees and from within through ecclesiastical traitors who do his bidding. One religion, however, has escaped his withering secularist gaze: Islam.

As he repeats incessantly, America is "not at war with Islam." The implication Obama leaves by this frequent comment is that his predecessor was at war with Islam, which is false. If anything, George W. Bush was much too soft and politically correct in his view of Islam. Bush dispatched his adviser Karen Hughes to the Islamic world as a goodwill ambassador to reassure Muslims that he saw Islam as a "religion of peace."

For Obama, the growth of doctrinal Christianity at home is more troubling than the spread of radical Islam abroad. His culture war with Christians is of far more interest to him than are the battles of Afghanistan. As America's new commander in chief, with forces engaged around the world fighting terrorism, Obama's priority was abolishing "Don't Ask, Don't Tell." As Obama noted, "Ending 'Don't Ask, Don't Tell' was a topic in my first meeting with Secretary Gates, Admiral Mullen, and the Joint Chiefs. We talked about how to end this policy. We talked about how success in both passing and implementing this change depended on working closely with the Pentagon. And that's what we did." Obama muscled the abolition of "Don't Ask, Don't Tell" through a lame-duck session of Congress after his party got clocked in the November 2010 elections. Joe Biden was so excited by the policy's repeal that he declared it "inevitable" that opposition to gay marriage would collapse too (thus foreshadowing his 2012 endorsement of gay marriage).

Obama's approach to Islam is one of tolerance and accommodation, even as he steps up his stiff-arming of Christians. Imagine if he treated Muslims as heavy-handedly as he treats pro-life Catholic doctors, nurses, and pharmacists, who are supposed to check their consciences at the hospital door. Imagine if he was as dismissive of imams and sheikhs as he is of pro-life priests, pastors, and rabbis whose concerns about the sanctity of human life are treated as a "war on women." Imagine if he imposed regulatory decrees on mosques, madrassas, and Islamic charities similar to his HHS mandate. Surely Islamic groups like CAIR would erupt in fury, accuse him of rank persecution, and unleash lawyers on his administration. They would probably call his behavior an incitement to "holy war."

By the secularist standards of the ACLU, Barack Obama's enthusiasm for Islam violates the "separation of church and state." But somehow his secularist allies don't mind that he holds "Iftar dinners" at the White House, gushes about Islam as a great and blameless religion, and treats the Koran with a reverence he never extends to, say, St. Paul's Letter to the Romans (Obama once dismissed it as "obscure," since it contains a condemnation of sodomy).

Obama's boosterism for Islam could be termed Islamophilia. At times his cheerleading for it has surpassed even the satirical imagination of *Onion* writers. In 2010, for example, NASA administrator Charles Bolden announced that the space program had adopted a groundbreaking new mission—to serve as a self-esteem project for global Islam. Bolden informed a reporter with Al Jazeera that when he took the NASA job, Obama made it clear to him that "perhaps foremost, he wanted to find a way to reach out to the Muslim world and engage much more with dominantly Muslim nations to help them feel good about their historic contribution to science…and math and engineering."

Taxpayers were astonished to learn that Obama conceived of America's space program as a learning annex for Muslims suffering from melancholy. How radical Muslims throughout the world who consider science intrinsically blasphemous would respond to this therapy is a matter Bolden didn't explain to reporters. Still, the policy fit with the overall political correctness of this administration: where others see terrorists, Obama sees misguided peace activists; where others see tormentors of scholars, he sees budding space engineers.

But lost on Bolden and Obama was the reason imams don't "feel good" about Islam's centuries-back contribution to science: today's mainstream Islamic theology views science as inescapably impious; it considers the assumption of scientifically detectable predictability in the universe a limitation on God's freedom and transcendence. This confused theology has effectively killed science in the Islamic world, which is why its countries produce almost no patents or scientific texts. Yet these are the countries with which the Obama administration hopes to one day coordinate tricky space flights—a quixotic if not dangerous hope that comes from the same president who boasts of the Democrats as the party "of science" and routinely blasts Christians as hidebound opponents of it.

Obama's Islamophilia extends well beyond NASA. It extends to his Justice Department, where Eric Holder initially planned to give a civilian jury trial to the Muslim planners of 9/11, and where he refuses to let his aides identify radical Islam as a terrorist motive. It extends to his National Security Council, where John Brennan endorses the concept of jihad as a harmless mode of self-improvement. It extends to his military where top brass fretted over the possible loss of "diversity" as part of the backlash after the Fort Hood shooting by a jihadist.

RAMADAN DINNERS AT THE WHITE HOUSE

Obama's sympathy for Islam is near bottomless and has resulted in grimly comic propaganda from the White House. Consider, for example, its self-reporting at WhiteHouse.gov after one of Obama's much-ballyhooed Ramadan dinners: "Last night, President Obama continued the White House tradition of hosting an Iftar—the meal that breaks the day of fasting—celebrating Ramadan in the State Dining Room."

A tradition? The White House was using the word loosely, to say the least, referring not to a continuous presidential practice, but to the fact, left intentionally vague, that during his war negotiations with Tunisian envoy Sidi Soliman Mellimelli, President Thomas Jefferson held a Ramadan dinner for him, but not for the reasons Obama implied.

Desperate to end the Barbary War with Islamic pirates, Jefferson had invited Mellimelli to Washington for negotiations. According to historian Gaye Wilson, the visit put Jefferson and his staff in an awkward spot: James Madison, then the secretary of State, had to field Mellimelli's request for "concubines." Jefferson humored Mellimelli, instructing White House aides to keep in mind that peace with the Barbary pirates required passing "unnoticed the irregular conduct of their ministers." The war negotiations dragged on and then happened to coincide with Ramadan. Consequently, a scheduled dinner at the White House had to be moved back from "half after three" to "precisely at sunset" in order for Mellimelli to attend, according to Wilson.

Jefferson was hardly starting a White House "tradition." He was under no illusions about the militant character of Islam.

Obama has also made misleading references to the "Koran" Jefferson owned, as if Jefferson had purchased it for religious edification. The truth is that Jefferson purchased it for self-protection: he wanted to understand the attitudes and war tactics of the Barbary pirates; Jefferson saw the Koran as a manual for war.

Perhaps the intensity of Obama's Islamophilia explains the persistence with which some Americans still view him as a Muslim, according to polls. This story pops up from time to time in the press. These Americans assume that the president must be Islamic, since he speaks of his "Muslim roots" with such gusto, says he hails from "generations of Muslims," has written about being born to a line of Muslim males, went to a Muslim school in Islamic Indonesia, speaks glowingly of Islam whenever he gets the chance, holds Ramadan dinners in the White House, tells his NASA head to turn the space agency into a Muslim outreach program, and mistreats doctrinal Christians routinely.

These Americans are wrong. Obama is not a Muslim. He is a nominal Christian. But it is fair to say that their confusion stems in part from the mixed signals Obama has sent.

Ironically, this false suspicion was fed originally not by Republicans but by Obama's fellow Democrats. It was Hillary Clinton who slyly said that Obama isn't a Muslim "as far as I know," which was widely inter- preted as a doubt-raising tactic. It was Hillary's campaign that allegedly sent to the *Drudge Report* an image of Obama in Muslim garb. It was Hillary's consultant Mark Penn who wrote internal memos, which were later leaked, saying that he couldn't "imagine America electing a president during a time of war who is not at his center fundamentally American in his thinking and in his values."

This represents Obama's most significant weakness, Penn counseled Hillary Clinton. He suggested that she give speeches about how she was "born in the middle of America to the middle class in the middle of the last century" as a way to draw a contrast with Obama's non-Western upbringing.

Penn's advice explains why Hillary appeared to pause when asked by Steve Kroft of *60 Minutes* if she thought Obama was a Muslim and why she used the hedging phrase, "as far as I know," when she finally said no. This pausing was designed to leave Americans with the lingering question: Should we entrust the war on terror to someone who might share the enemy's religion? Under Penn's tutelage, Hillary was trying hard to portray herself as a patriotic, even Christian, American running against a less-than-patriotic, possibly Muslim opponent who was not terribly committed to the war on terror. In one of the debates, Hillary even seized on Louis Farrakhan's endorsement of Obama, forcing him to disavow the "Nation of Islam." Meanwhile, she was sending Bill and Chelsea to Christian churches, and her staffers were appearing on television shows wearing Christian crosses. During the Texas primary, she dispatched Bill and Chelsea to Joel Osteen's Christian mega-church in Houston to accentuate her Christian credentials.

Sensing that a smear was underway, Obama fended it off by repeatedly calling himself a "devout Christian," by pouting that he had inherited his faith from his mother, a "Christian from Kansas," and by asserting angrily that he had taken his senatorial oath on the "family bible." This was all balderdash: his Mom was an atheistic Ford Foundation-affiliated anthropologist who never believed in, let alone practiced, Christianity. Nor did Obama's maternal grandparents practice Christianity, though they did for a short time attend a Unitarian Church in Washington State associated with enough Communists to earn a very odd nickname: "The Dunhams sometimes attended the East Shore Unitarian Church, which was jokingly known around town as the 'Little Red Church on the Hill.'

But religion was hardly paramount in the Dunham household. Ann usually spoke of herself as an atheist," wrote Obama biographer David Remnick.

Once Hillary and McCain were defeated and he was safely ensconced in the White House, Obama resumed his Islamophilia. In his first year in office, he flew to Cairo for a major overture to the Islamic world. He tried to wow his audience by saying that he came from "generations of Muslims" and that he had spent "several years" of his childhood in Islamic Indonesia, where he "heard the call of the azaan at the break of dawn and at the fall of dusk."

Obama's Islamophilia strikes many as particularly odd since it doesn't even involve the promotion of Islam's moderate variants. A persistent complaint from secularists active in the "Arab Spring" is that the Obama administration tends to side with Islamic theocrats over them.

In 2009, the *Washington Post* ran an intriguing story about Obama's unwillingness to help moderate Muslims lest that upset the hardline imams who run the religion. The story's title was, "As Indonesia debates Islam's role, U.S. stays out: Post-9/11 push to boost moderates gives way," and started with an anecdote about how a Ford Foundation employee rejected a scholar in the early 1980s seeking funds to promote moderate Islam. "He left empty handed. The United States, he was told, was 'not interested in getting into Islam.'"

The Ford Foundation employee was Barack Obama's mother, "Ann Dunham, a U.S. anthropologist who lived in Indonesia for more than a decade." The story went on to say that today "U.S. thinking has moved back toward what it was in Dunham's day: stay out of Islam."

Under Obama, the White House has undermined moderate Muslims while averting its gaze from violent ones. Self-identified Muslim terrorists have shot up a military base at Fort Hood, tried to blow up a plane over Detroit on the day of Jesus Christ's birth, and attempted to bomb tourists in Times Square. Yet U.S. Attorney General Eric Holder prides himself on refusing to identify radical Islam as a motive for terrorism, and Obama security adviser John Brennan holds that jihad is a concept of self-improvement that Oprah could endorse. It is "a legitimate tenet of Islam, meaning to purify oneself or one's community," Brennan has said.

Has Brennan shared his understanding of Islam with the imams who issue death edicts and call for violent jihad? They probably wouldn't regard his definition of jihad as exactly authoritative. But then again, they are probably happy that the Obama administration has finally found a religion it considers "holy"—not Christianity, which it regards as a malign force in public life, but Islam, which it considers intrinsically peaceful.

Obama's absurd Islamophilia has worsened America's relationship with Israel. Obama is forever condemning Israel for this or that act of "brutality" even as he calls Islam a "religion of peace." In 2010, the Obama administration condemned Israeli soldiers for supposedly roughing up peace activists on a Gaza flotilla. The Illinois pol who launched his political career from the living room of a domestic terrorist (Bill Ayers) has trouble identifying foreign ones. Video footage of the encounter between the Israeli soldiers and the "peace activists" on the flotilla exposed the folly of the Obama administration's knee-jerk criticism of the Israeli commandos: it showed that the self-described "peace activists" were wielding knives and had begun their journey with a song about "Khaybar," according to British journalist Melanie Phillips. Khaybar is a reference to Islam's version of peace activism in the seventh century, when Muslims slaughtered Jews in an oasis town near Medina. "Khaybar, Khaybar o Jews, the army of Muhammad will return," goes the Arabic chant.

According to John Brennan, "remaining faithful to our values requires something else—that we never surrender the diversity and tolerance and openness to different cultures and faiths that define us as

Americans." Too bad this doesn't include respect for Christianity and Judaism.

REFLEXIVE ISLAMOPHILIA

Gary Bauer, the former presidential candidate who now runs the group American Values, told us that "America's frayed friendship with Israel under Obama stems from his indifference to Biblical lands" and Obama's reflexive support for Islam.

"Obama acts as if Israel building homes for Jews in Jerusalem is the biggest obstacle to peace in the Middle East. Meanwhile, he has no problem defending the construction of the Ground Zero mosque," said Bauer. "And his State Department saw no problem in spending taxpayer money to send Ground Zero mosque Imam Feisal Abdul Rauf to the Middle East on a goodwill tour."

"We know Obama attracted the votes of more than 9 in 10 Muslim American voters in 2008. And it's not because of Obama's support for gays in the military or abortion on demand. A major reason why is they knew under Obama, America's relationship with Israel would decline as would America's stature in the world."

The more irrational and non-Western a religion, the more Obama tends to like it. In fact, the self-described "rationalist" Obama treats the largest and most intellectually grounded religion in the world, Catholicism, as a dangerous superstition while accommodating dubious and zany non-Western sects. Did you know that Obama permits American Indians to kill bald eagles for religious purposes? Yes, not even his environmentalism stops him from preening as a "multicultural" admirer of non-Western religions. In March 2012, Obama's U.S. Fish and Wildlife Service granted a permit to the Northern Arapaho Tribe in Wyoming to kill two bald eagles so that they could have feathers for use in their Sun Dance.

Obama appears to see himself as the cosmopolitan dilettante who stands above all religions and judges their "rationality" by their usefulness to the socialist utopia to come. Islam is a flawless religion by his lights, while Christianity, unless it assumes the platform of the Democratic Party and sees Jesus Christ as a forerunner to Saul Alinsky, is dangerously bigoted and an impediment to "progress." Obama's America has a friend in Islam, but Christians can be "un-American," as Obama supporter Tom Hanks once described Christian proponents of traditional marriage in California.

The reason for the love liberals like Obama have for these non-Western religions goes beyond the childish and self-hating affinity of Western liberals for anything that undercuts the traditional moral foundations of the West. In fact, Western liberalism is attached to irrationality. Having ruptured a once-harmonious relationship between reason and religion in their own culture, Western liberals can't seem to stop themselves from championing similar ruptures in alien ones.

By different routes of irrationality, Western liberals and militant Muslims arrive at the same spot. Western liberals reach it by a distorted "reason" without faith, militant Muslims by a distorted "faith" without reason, with each imbalance producing its own culture of death: abortion and euthanasia in the West, jihad in the East.

An old-style liberal like the late Oriana Fallaci found it amazing that Enlightenment liberals could defend so enthusiastically the gross illiberal tendencies of militant Muslims and puzzled over how two seemingly different groups could turn up on the same side in debates. But it is not surprising if one considers their shared rejection of reason properly understood and the common enemy that rouses them—a lingering Christianity in the West.

Behind Obama's speeches pandering to the Muslim world (given in Indonesia, Egypt, and Turkey, among other places) is a deep sympathy for Islam that Obama would never extend to traditional Christianity.

As Obama geared up to abolish the conscience rights of Christian pro-lifers at American hospitals, as he used executive orders to force Christians to finance abortions at home and abroad, as he refused to support the law of the land defending traditional marriage (and his supporters placed Christian opponents of gay marriage in the moral category of racists), he was telling Muslims in Turkey, for example, that "America is not and never will be at war with Islam" and that America accepted the moderation of Muslims without question.

Obama droned on, apparently unaware that Turkish Christians were banned from opening churches and running seminaries and that they had been thrown into jail for insulting "Turkishness" after giving open witness to Jesus Christ; or that Sufi Muslims, who see themselves as moderates, were actually being persecuted.

None of this was worrisome to Obama, because his enemy is not Islam abroad, but Christianity at home. As far as Obama is concerned, the only religion to be "reformed"—which is to say destroyed—is the faith that shaped the West, not the religion of the West's historic adversary. Obama has in effect declared to Christians in America: either bring your understanding of Christianity into line with my liberalism or don't bother entering the public square. You want federal money? Well then, perform abortions, distribute condoms, and hire homosexual activists. He would never dare talk to Muslims in those terms. He gives back ancestral swords to freed Muslims from Guantanamo Bay and hands abortionists' forceps to Christian doctors.

CHAPTER EIGHT

"THE FIRST GAY PRESIDENT"

In May 2012, *Newsweek* ran a cover photo of Barack Obama, crowned with a halo. "The First Gay President," beamed the headline below the photo. The smugness and delusion of the liberal elite had reached new heights with this magazine cover. A boast the Founding Fathers would have considered a baffling insult was welcomed by the White House as proof of Obama's rectitude.

The press oohed and ahhed for days over the new "civil right" Obama had discovered. Reporters rolled out a flattering narrative about how his endorsement of gay marriage came through slow and pained "evolution." Obama, according to White House aides, planned to announce his support for it before the Democrats' convention in Charlotte. But the irrepressible Joe Biden had forced him to announce it earlier than expected after the vice president declared on *Meet the Press* that "men marrying men and women marrying women" struck him as laudable.

This account is naïve at best and lying drivel at worst. To anyone paying close attention, Obama's opposition to gay marriage was always a fiction—a position explained not by sincere philosophical considerations but by rawly political ones.

In fact, Obama had endorsed gay marriage almost a generation before. During his first run for office in 1996 as a state Senate candidate in Illinois, he had told a gay magazine based on Chicago's North Side, via a letter sent in reply to an issues survey, that he supported gay marriage: "I favor legalizing same-sex marriages, and would fight any effort to prohibit such marriages." Obama had signed the letter himself, but his staffers would later lie about the survey and pass his answer off as a miscommunication. The candidate, they insisted to reporters, opposed gay marriage.

Obama wasn't the only Democrat playing this deceptive game in the 1990s. After conservative Republicans bloodied his nose in 1994 and took back the House of Representatives, Bill Clinton had to feign an interest in "traditional values." His consultant Dick Morris quickly taught him how to play an opponent of gay marriage on TV. Out of this phoniness came Clinton's hasty signing of the Defense of Marriage Act, which the Democrats, as the country came to see, had no intention of enforcing. An anxious Clinton told the press during his 1996 reelection campaign: "I remain opposed to same-sex marriage. I believe marriage is an institution for the union of a man and a woman. This has been my long-standing position, and it is not being reviewed or reconsidered."

It didn't take long for Clinton, once safely out of office in 2000, to begin the process of reviewing and reconsidering it. Clinton unburdened himself of his true thoughts about gay marriage once he no longer had any races to run. "I personally support people doing what they want to do," he told the press. "I think it's wrong for someone to stop someone else from doing that."

THE CHARADE ENDS

"We'll get there," Teresa Heinz Kerry, the wife of John Kerry, promised gay activists in San Francisco back in 2004, even as her husband pretended to oppose gay marriage. The country, she said, was "evolving," and the Democrats would evolve with it. Time has proven her right, as a rash of Democrats now judge that the political and cultural climate is ripe for an endorsement of a position they always believed. Democratic pollsters who once cautioned liberal pols not to support gay marriage now inform them that they are more likely to pay a political price for opposing it than touting it. Andrew Cuomo became the hip new Democrat in 2011 after he successfully engineered the passage of gay marriage in New York State. A Catholic Democrat, Cuomo's slamdunking of secularism over the bishops inspired the Catholic Martin O'Malley to push gay marriage against feckless bishops in Maryland.

Obama has joined this charade, finding it easier to say that his view has "evolved" than to confess opportunistic deception for decades. Clinton said that his view suddenly changed once he left office due to his exposure to the edifying learning experience of watching his homosexual friends take care of tots. Obama has adopted the same fib. He told ABC's Robin Roberts that his mind suddenly changed after meeting the adopted children of homosexuals who go to school with his daughters. (What a sheltered president. Had he never met the adopted children of homosexuals before his daughters introduced him to a few?)

Obama had learned from Saul Alinsky to use caution when pursuing projects of social engineering. One must turn the hot water up gradually in the pot, so to speak, lest your specimens jump out. Grasping this lesson, Obama in 2008 said that he supported "robust civil unions." The addition of "robust" to "civil unions" allowed him to maintain at once his nominal opposition to gay marriage while signaling to gay activists that he was inching towards an endorsement.

Like John Kerry, Obama went through the rigamarole of saying in debates that he opposed gay marriage. But in his heart he didn't. And anyone paying close attention could see that his deeds contradicted his words. Even during the 2008 race, he was sending out letters to gay-rights activists congratulating them on their new marriage licenses. He was describing Bill Clinton's/Dick Morris's Defense of Marriage act as reactionary and unconstitutional. He was sending his wife out to applaud gay-rights activists for torpedoing gay-marriage bans.

The insincerity of his opposition to gay marriage was also detectable in his memoirs. The construction of his position on gay marriage in *The Audacity of Hope* is comically passive, salted with a series of weak qualifiers: "In years hence I may be seen as someone who was on the wrong side of history" and "I was reminded that it is my obligation not only as an elected official in a pluralistic society, but also as a Christian, to remain open to the possibility that my unwillingness to support gay marriage is misguided."

As president, he immediately invited the gay activists who helped elect him to "LGBT" receptions at the White House, where he assured them that crusty Americans could one day be cajoled out of their "worn arguments and old attitudes." "Welcome to your White House," he burbled, promising to support every item on the LGBT agenda: "We've been in office six months now. I suspect that by the time this administration is over, I think you guys will have pretty good feelings about the Obama administration."

They do. Should Obama win a second term, the justices he appoints will almost certainly unveil a bogus new constitutional right to gay marriage, discovered within the "penumbras" of *Lawrence* v. *Texas*. At which point Obama, drawing upon the faux-pained honesty he has perfected, can regurgitate what he wrote in his memoirs: that he was once on "the wrong side of history" but has now happily come into the light.

Now that Obama supports gay marriage, does this mean he supports federalizing marriage (his stated reason for holding that DOMA is unconstitutional)? Of course it does. But he cravenly lied in his interview with Robin Roberts, saying that he considers it a "state" matter. This is Obama's latest limited modified hangout position. He doesn't even bother to coordinate his lies at this point: If gay marriage is a matter of "equality"—in other words, a right shared by all citizens no matter where they live—how could he truly believe gay marriage is a matter for "states" to decide? Does he consider segregation a "state" matter? Obviously, the logic of his support for gay marriage as a "right of equality" requires that he support federalizing gay marriage. But with typical cowardice and manipulation, he leaves this implicit stance vague so that he can win in 2012 and then unfurl it later in his second term. (Gay activists noticed this contradiction in his "endorsement" of gay marriage and expressed disappointment that he was still playing political games.)

In fact, the Democrats have supported a de facto federal right to gay marriage since the 1970s, when they endorsed the Equal Rights Amendment. Had the ERA passed, traditional marriage laws would have collapsed.

The embrace of gay marriage in Massachusetts shows how that would have happened. The majority opinion in *Goodridge* v. *Dept. of Public Health*, the 2003 Massachusetts Supreme Judicial Court case that brought gay marriage to the Bay State, was conveniently vague about how the Massachusetts Constitution could justify gay marriage. Since the Massachusetts Constitution was adopted in 1780, and written by John Adams, it is absurd to believe that its equality language could have included same-sex marriage. But the concurring opinion in *Goodridge* v. *Dept. of Public Health* cited the Massachusetts state Equal Rights Amendment as authority to legalize same-sex marriages. The state ERA was added to Article 1 of the Massachusetts Constitution in 1976. It provides: "Equality under the law shall not be denied or abridged because of sex, race, color, creed or national origin."

Judge Cordy's dissent (joined by both other dissenting judges) reminded the court that just before the 1976 election when the voters adopted the state ERA, the official Massachusetts commission, which was charged with the duty of advising the voters what ERA's effect would be, issued this statement: "An equal rights amendment will have no effect upon the allowance or denial of homosexual marriages. The equal rights amendment is not concerned with the relationship of two persons of the same sex; it only addresses those laws or public-related actions which treat persons of opposite sexes differently."

Boston newspapers echoed this disclaimer, labeling claims that the ERA would be the basis for same-sex marriage as "exaggerated" and "unfounded." Editorializing for ERA, the *Boston Globe* noted that "those urging a no vote...argue that the amendment would...legitimize marriage between people of the same sex. In reality, the proposed amendment would require none of these things."

Yet the *Goodridge* decision did use the Massachusetts ERA to legalize marriage between people of the same sex. UCLA law professor Eugene Volokh posted on his website: "Phyllis Schlafly said it would be like this." He cited typical examples from the liberal press ridiculing the opponents of ERA for "canards," "scare tactics," and "hysterics" in predicting that ERA would require same-sex marriage.

> *U.S. News & World Report* (April, 28, 1975): "Opponents, for example, suggested passage of ERA would mean abortion on demand, legalization of homosexual marriages, sex-integrated prisons and reform schools—all claims that were hotly denied by ERA supporters."

New York Times (July 5, 1981): "Discussion of [the ERA] bogged down in hysterical claims that the amendment would eliminate privacy in bathrooms, encourage homosexual marriage, put women in the trenches and deprive housewives of their husbands' support."

Washington Post (February 19, 1982): "The vote in Virginia [against the ERA] came after proponents argued on behalf of civil rights for women and opponents trotted out the old canards about homosexual marriages and unisex restrooms."

Volokh concluded: "So the Massachusetts ERA did contribute to constitutional protection for homosexual marriage—as the opponents of the ERA predicted, and as the supporters of the ERA vehemently denied."

OBAMA'S COMING REGIME OF FEDERAL GAY MARRIAGE

Under Obama's regime of federal gay marriage, one can expect violations of religious freedom to multiply, as they have in states like New York where gay marriage has become law. As the *Washington Times* reported, marriage clerks in New York are no longer free to abstain from signing gay marriage licenses. They have to sign them whether they like it or not:

To date, the most public religious impact of the Marriage Equality Act is the case of Barbara MacEwen, the longtime town clerk in Volney, N.Y.

Citing religious and moral objections, Ms. MacEwen asked to have the town's deputy clerk sign gay marriage licenses instead of herself. A state senator from another district responded by suggesting that Ms. MacEwen quit her job if she couldn't carry out her duties under the new law. She quickly agreed to sign all licenses.

Once homosexual behavior is blessed by the state through the privileged laws of marriage, any citizen, in government or out of government, who regards homosexual marriage as an affront to God or natural law is seen and treated as an enemy of the state. Where gay marriage exists, religious freedom quickly disappears.

Obama thinks himself very generous for noting that even after gay marriage becomes a state norm, religions will be able to determine their "own sacraments." How big of him. That's about as reassuring as Sebelius's standard for religious freedom in relation to the HHS mandate: that no woman would be forced to use contraceptives. "No individual will be forced to buy or use contraception," HHS announced as a way of showing its commitment to "religious freedom."

The Obama administration's standard of religious freedom consists of promises that the federal government won't bust down church doors and force priests to preside at gay marriages, and that it won't enter houses and inject women with contraceptives.

Of course, even that day may come. The idea of mandatory contraception has been bruited about at the state level for drug-abusing or welfare-abusing mothers; and it is not hard to imagine that with the federal government counting on Obamacare cost savings from contraception that it could become as mandatory as having health insurance. And if gay marriage really is a civil right, how long will the federal government allow churches to opt out from respecting it? Obama's supposed respect for the integrity of religious "sacraments" isn't worth taking seriously. Under the nanny state of the left, nothing remains "private" for long. Should Obama win a second term, one can imagine his friends at Planned Parenthood calling for forcible sterilizations to "save costs" and gay groups calling for "hate crime" fines to be levied on Catholic priests who refuse to bless gay unions.

Already in Canada and Western Europe, nonconformists can be dragged before judges for harboring the "wrong" thoughts. The French actress Brigitte Bardot has been "tried" several times for criticizing Islam. So was the late author Oriana Fallaci, who stood trial in Italy for "defaming Islam."

Do not kid yourselves: it could happen here. In a second term, the Obama administration will bring that day much closer.

CHAPTER NINE

OBAMA'S SECULARIZED MILITARY

In the early fall of 2010, Admiral Michael Mullen, then-chairman of the Joint Chiefs of Staff, gave a briefing to a Special Forces unit at Fort Bragg in North Carolina. During the question-and-answer session, a chaplain opposed to the repeal of "Don't Ask, Don't Tell" asked Mullen if traditionally Christian chaplains would be "protected" after the ban. Would they be allowed to continue to teach that homosexuality is morally wrong? No, replied Mullen. "If you cannot get in line, resign your commission," he told the chaplain.

This captures the rawly intolerant spirit of Barack Obama's secularized military. Under the Obama administration, military chaplains lose their First Amendment rights. Simply put, chaplains who don't share Obama's gay rights agenda need not apply. They are no longer welcome in his military.

Needless to say, privates who object to the gay agenda have even less of a future in Obama's military than conservative military chaplains. As the *Washington Times* reported in 2010, Lieutenant General Thomas

P. Bostick, the Army's deputy chief of staff in charge of personnel, addressing U.S. soldiers in Germany, said that objecting soldiers should "get out": "Unfortunately, we have a minority of service members who are still racists and bigoted and you will never be able to get rid of all of them. . . . But these people opposing this new policy will need to get with the program, and if they can't, they need to get out."

In researching this book we heard stories of chaplains losing promotions over acts as minor as forwarding emails containing links to articles critical of gay rights. On Obama's animal farm, some military chaplains are more equal than others. Chaplains who reject the historic teaching of Christianity on the sinfulness of homosexual acts can expect a career rise; chaplains who follow traditional Christian teaching can expect demotions.

Even before the announcement of Obama's open support for gay marriage, we heard rumbles of fear from military chaplains about what might happen in Obama's second term. "I liken the current cultural war to guerrilla warfare," said one. The first term was only a "lull," but in the second "we will see a major attack."

But, as Elaine Donnelly, head of the Center for Military Readiness, has pointed out, what happened in Obama's first term has been bad enough. "At the present time, rights of conscience are protected only for the minority of chaplains who support the mandates of LGBT law and related policies. This is not adequate, because others who support traditional marriage also should have protected rights of conscience under the U.S. Constitution, which authorizes the chaplaincy to provide for religious expression among troops fighting far from home."

For chaplains who wish to preach orthodox Christianity anywhere beyond their pulpit—and probably in time not even there—persecution and career oblivion are guaranteed.

"The only option for chaplains who wish to express religious convictions in settings other than worship, such as educational/family programs and marriage counseling, is to revoke their sponsoring agency's endorsement and receive an honorable discharge if they are eligible to leave. Such policies are already imposing a chilling effect on chaplains," Donnelly has written.

In his lawless defiance of the Defense of Marriage Act, Obama has used his first term to transform the military into an instrument of propaganda for gay rights. This includes the use of military bases for DOMA-violating gay marriage ceremonies, which has forced military lawyers to find ways to skirt the law by authorizing "private ceremonies," not specifying marriage, conducted by chaplains not acting with the official endorsement of the Defense Department.

As commander in chief, Obama, in the pursuit of secularizing the military and advancing the gay agenda, is acting like the generalissimo of a military junta, openly disobeying the rule of law and pressuring his generals to flout the Defense of Marriage Act passed by Congress, not to mention violate traditional First Amendment rights that have been accorded military chaplains.

As Elaine Donnelly has written, "Congress should not allow administration officials to keep changing the definition and character of marriage in the military, in order to fulfill President Obama's political promises to LGBT (lesbian, gay, bisexual, transgender) activists. Before the administration implements flawed social policies that weaken marriage, divide the chaplain corps, impose incalculable costs, and undermine military culture and morale, members of Congress need to assert their constitutional right to make policy for the armed forces."

The semantic games to which Donnelly refers above were due to a fiasco in April 2011 when the Navy Chief of Chaplains issued a memorandum authorizing training for gay marriage ceremonies on military bases. To his embarrassment, his baldly written memo had to be withdrawn, as it too obviously violated DOMA. "If the base is located in a state where same-sex marriage is legal, then the base facilities may be used to celebrate the marriage," wrote Rear Admiral Mark L. Tidd, the Chief of Navy Chaplains. Republican congressmen were furious at the news of his memo. "This new guidance from the Navy clearly violates the law," said Congressman Todd Akin, the chairman of the House Armed Services Seapower Subcommittee. "While our president may not like this law, it is unbelievable that our Navy would issue guidance that clearly violates this law. While a state may legalize same-sex marriage, federal property and federal employees, like Navy chaplains, should not be used to perform marriages that are not recognized by federal law."

Since then, Obama has promised to veto any legislation by House Republicans that seeks to prevent DOMA-violating gay marriage ceremonies on military bases or that seeks to protect the religious freedom of military chaplains. White House officials have issued aggressive veto warnings of these bills, saying that such legislation poses a threat to "good order and discipline" and that it would constitute "unconstitutional" discrimination according to "sexual orientation."

Defense Department Counsel Jeh C. Johnson claims that chaplains still enjoy religious freedom, but he uses very careful and narrow language while doing so. The abolition of the ban on active homosexuals in the military, he testified before Congress, "would not require a chaplain to change what he preaches—what he counsels in the religious context." Notice those last four words—"in the religious context." In other words, if a chaplain objects to Obama's gay rights agenda anywhere outside of the pulpit he will be punished. And even a chaplain's words from the pulpit can get him in trouble. Look what happened to Catholic chaplains after the HHS mandate came down.

SILENCED

A sign of what Obama has in mind for military chaplains—namely, silencing any of them that disagree with his new Brave New World morality—appeared shortly after the announcement of his HHS mandate when the military prohibited Catholics priests from condemning it in homilies. Archbishop Timothy Broglio, head of the archdiocese for the military services, had told Catholic military chaplains to read a letter during Masses protesting the HHS mandate. But they were ordered by the military not to do so from the pulpit. The office of the Chief of Chaplains of the U.S. Army forbade an oral reading of the letter. Archbishop Timothy Broglio had written in it that "the Administration has cast aside the First Amendment to the Constitution of the United States" in a way that is "denying Catholics our Nation's first and most fundamental freedom, that of religious liberty."

The archdiocese for the military services publicized the military's silencing of Catholic chaplains:

On Thursday, January 26, Archbishop Broglio emailed a pastoral letter to Catholic military chaplains with instructions that it be read from the pulpit at Sunday Masses the following weekend in all military chapels. The letter calls on Catholics to resist the policy initiative, recently affirmed by the United States Department of Health and Human Services, for federally mandated health insurance covering sterilization, abortifacients and contraception, because it represents a violation of the freedom of religion recognized by the U.S. Constitution.

The Army's Office of the Chief of Chaplains subsequently sent an email to senior chaplains advising them that the Archbishop's letter was not coordinated with that office and asked that it not be read from the pulpit. The Chief's office directed that the letter was to be mentioned in the Mass announcements and distributed in printed form in the back of the chapel.

Archbishop Broglio and the Archdiocese stand firm in the belief, based on legal precedent, that such a directive from the Army constituted a violation of his Constitutionally-protected right of free speech and the free exercise of religion, as well as those same rights of all military chaplains and their congregants.

Some priests and pastors are worried that they will not only lose control over their pulpits but also their chapel spaces. As one chaplain said to us, "Will the Department of Defense be able to override what happens in our chapels?" According to a September 2011 memo from DOD general counsel Johnson on the "uses of DOD facilities," any chapel space could potentially be turned into a setting for a gay marriage. The memo reads in part:

> Determinations regarding use of DOD real property and facilities for private functions, including religious and other ceremonies, should be made on a sexual-orientation neutral basis, provided such use is not prohibited by applicable state and local laws.

In 2011, Elaine Donnelly received copies of some of the Department of Defense's training materials for those not yet reconciled to Obama's gay-friendly military. The materials are clearly designed to scare conservative chaplains into submission.

"CMR [the Council for Military Readiness] has obtained copies of the 'Tier One' training documents that the various services are already using to 're-educate' the troops," wrote Donnelly. "The training program for Army chaplains, in particular, makes it very clear that dissenters will have no option but to leave the service, if they are eligible and if they do not owe time to the Army."

Here are the most chilling passages from the training materials:

> You may hear the language, "Gay, Lesbian, Bisexual", or "GLB" at certain times in reference to homosexual Soldiers. As of today the Army has not directed the use of the any [*sic*] specific reference term but has accepted the usage of these terms.
>
> You may, in appropriate circumstances and within the limitations of law and policy, express your moral or religious beliefs regarding sexual orientation. However, you may NOT make statements detrimental to good order and discipline and must obey lawful orders. You do NOT have the right to refuse duty or duty assignments based on a moral objection to another's sexual orientation.
>
> You remain obligated to follow orders that involve interaction with others who are homosexual even if an unwillingness to do so is based on strong, sincerely held moral or religious beliefs. As expressed in the Manual for Courts-Martial regarding a Soldier's obligation to obey orders: "the dictates of a person's conscience, religion, or personal philosophy cannot justify or excuse the disobedience of an otherwise lawful order."

Should Obama win a second term, expect resistant conservative Christian chaplains to be court-martialed.

CHAPTER TEN

TEACHING "SOCIAL JUSTICE"

O bama is clearly counting in 2012 on one of the demographic groups that turned out for him in large numbers in 2008—young people. And why should young people support Barack Obama, a president who has presided over policies that have seen youth unemployment skyrocket?

One big reason is the education they have been given—and that includes the education given to young evangelicals and Catholics in the public schools, the schools that nearly 90 percent of students attend. Obama in 2008 won double the percentage of the young evangelical votes that went for John Kerry in 2004. And if you asked these young evangelicals themselves why they voted for Obama, you might hear "hope" or "change," but you would also hear "social justice." "Social justice" is more important to these children of the so-called "religious right" than the prime moral issues of abortion and same-sex unions, even though, whether they know it or not, social justice is simply left-wing jargon for the agenda of Alinskyite revolutionaries. But it is effective, and Obama's allies have been peddling it for decades in the public schools.

In the 1980s, many radical anti-war activists of the 1960s and 1970s acquired a new identity and became tenured college professors. Among them was Obama's friend William Ayers, a founder of the infamous Weather Underground, the organization that set bombs in public buildings such as the U.S. Capitol and the Pentagon.

Ayers escaped prosecution only because of government misconduct in collecting evidence against him. Ayers later boasted: "Guilty as hell. Free as a bird." In a remarkable coincidence, Ayers was quoted in the *New York Times* on the morning of 9/11 as saying, "I don't regret setting bombs. I feel we didn't do enough." Later that week, Ayers was quoted in the *New York Times Magazine* as saying, "This society is not a just and fair and decent place."

Ayers enrolled in Columbia Teachers College, where he picked up a Ph.D. and emerged as a professor of education at the University of Illinois at Chicago. He launched a new career, directing his revolutionary energy into changing classroom curricula instead of setting bombs.

Ayers's political views are as radical now as they were in the 1970s. "Viva President Chavez!" he exclaimed in a speech in Venezuela in 2006, in which he also declared, "Education is the motor-force of revolution."

Ayers, and his numerous ideological allies and progenitors— including the massively influential "father of modern education" John Dewey, a socialist and signer of the Humanist Manifesto—have been on a decades-long mission to transform public education into anti-American indoctrination and to get young people to demand that government control the economy, politics, and culture. We saw the result in 2008 post-election surveys: seven out of every ten voters between the ages of eighteen and twenty-nine now favor expanding the role of government, and agree that the government should do more to solve the nation's problems. It's obvious which party and which candidates will get their vote.

One might assume that Ayers's peculiar resumé would put him on the outer fringe of the left-wing education establishment. Not so. Ayers developed a large following as he taught resentment against America. In 2008, he was elected by his peers as vice president for curriculum of the American Education Research Association, the nation's largest organization of education professors and researchers.

From his post as professor of education, William Ayers became a leading advocate of "social justice" teaching, i.e., getting students to believe that they are victims of an unjust, oppressive, and racist America. After a few years of this indoctrination, young people are ripe targets for community organizers to mobilize them to vote and carry out "hope and change" or what Ayers would call "revolution."

The National Association of Scholars reports that the term "social justice" is today understood to mean "the advocacy of more egalitarian access to income through state-sponsored redistribution." That is academic verbiage for Barack Obama's assertion that he wants to "spread the wealth around."

David Horowitz of the California-based David Horowitz Freedom Center is more blunt. He says that "social justice" teaching is "shorthand for opposition to American traditions of individual justice and free-market economics." He says it teaches students that "American society is an inherently 'oppressive' society that is 'systemically' racist, 'sexist,' and 'classist' and thus discriminates institutionally against women, non-whites, working Americans, and the poor."

On October 29, 2008, the pro-public-school-establishment journal *Education Week* featured a long front-page article describing "social-justice teaching." This article provides ample evidence that "social-justice teaching" should be a major concern to everyone who cares what the next generation is taught with taxpayers' money.

Education Week defines "social-justice teaching" as "teaching kids to question whoever happens to hold the reins of power at a particular moment. It's about seeing yourself not just as a consumer [of informa-tion], but as an actor-critic" in the world around you. This revealing explanation comes from the words of Bill Bigelow, the curriculum editor of a Milwaukee-based organization called Rethinking Schools, which publishes instructional materials relating to issues of race and equity.

The purpose of Rethinking Schools instructional materials is to teach teachers how to "weave social justice issues throughout the cur-riculum." Lessons include "Rethinking Mathematics: Teaching Social Justice by the Numbers," which shows teachers ways to "weave social justice issues throughout the mathematics curriculum," and "Reading, Writing, and Rising Up: Teaching About Social Justice and the Power of the Written Word."

Bigelow assigns students to role-play various oppressed groups in foreign countries. Students can easily infer that Americans are oppressed like people in foreign countries, and most young people have no store of information with which to rebut this propaganda.

THE "PEDAGOGY OF THE OPPRESSED"

"Social-justice" lessons concentrate on past mistakes in U.S. history rather than on our many remarkable accomplishments and opportuni-ties. Emphasizing problems and injustices rather than achievements is given the pretentious label "critical pedagogy."

"Social-justice teaching" does not mean justice as most Americans understand the term. Those who use the term make clear that it means the United States is an unjust and oppressive society, and that the solution is for community organizers to organize the poor and minorities to demonstrate and to demand political power so they will be given govern-ment handouts.

Education Week identifies the "special-interest groups" that promote "social-justice teaching" and provide curricular materials, online resources, and "professional development" (conferences and seminars to indoctrinate teachers). These groups include an affiliate of the American Educational Research Association, the Cambridge-based Educators for Social Responsibility, and the Washington-based Teaching for Change, in addition to Rethinking Schools.

The lobbyists for "social-justice teaching" and "critical pedagogy" sponsor conferences to mold the thinking of teachers, which are well-attended at taxpayers' expense. Teachers 4 Social Justice attracted 1,000 educators to an October 2008 seminar in Berkeley, California.

The National Association for Multicultural Education (NAME) sponsors seminars with sessions entitled "Our Work as Social Justice Educators," "Teaching for Social Justice in Elementary Schools," "Dismantling White Privilege and Supporting Anti-Racist Education in our Classrooms and Schools," "Talking About Religious Oppression and Christian Privilege," and "Creating Change Agents Who Teach for Social Justice."

School boards and principals allocate large amounts of money for teachers to receive this type of so-called "professional development." Registration for NAME's November 2008 conference in New Orleans cost $375 per NAME member or $475 per non-member, in addition to airfare and hotel expense.

Lesson plans are available from a 30-year-old magazine called *Radical Teacher*, which was founded as "a socialist, feminist, and anti-racist journal on the theory and practice of teaching."

Education schools are lining up behind "social justice" teaching and forcing it on aspiring teachers so they will adopt politically correct liberal attitudes and character traits. At Humboldt State University in northern California, Professor Gayle Olson-Raymer teaches the social studies methods class, which is required for prospective high school history and social studies teachers. Her syllabus states: "It is not an option for history teachers to teach social justice and social responsibility; it is a mandate."

When a teacher engages in this type of advocacy in lieu of teaching literature, math, history, or science, the teacher is engaging in political indoctrination.

Some "social justice" professional development seminars have urged teachers to begin inculcating "correct" sociopolitical attitudes in children as young as age two because it is so easy to impose their views on children who enter school at such a young age.

Professor Ayers declined to be interviewed for the *Education Week* article. His comments were unnecessary since the article was generally favorable to "social-justice teaching" and dismissive of its critics.

"Social justice" is certainly not a new concept, but left-wing educators have redefined the term to mean teaching for "social justice" by overthrowing the current money and power structure. *Education Week* identifies this new meaning of "social justice" as coming from the writings of the late Brazilian educator, Paulo Freire. His best-known book, *Pedagogy of the Oppressed* (1970), is considered a classic text of radical education theory and is regularly assigned in education schools.

Paulo Freire developed his liberation pedagogy out of his experience with illiterate peasants in northeastern Brazil, who probably were victims of a semifeudal society. But Brazilian oppression has no relation to the U.S. economic or social structure, and it is dishonest to pretend that it is relevant to educating minority children in the United States.

A survey made of the principal books used in the basic "foundations of education" and "methods" courses in the most prestigious schools of education discovered that the most frequently used books were those of Paolo Freire and William Ayers.

After Freire's theories indoctrinated teachers in teachers' colleges, his notions made their way into public schools, especially where low-income and minority kids can be taught what is colloquially called Oppression

Studies. It is easy to find schools that specialize in "social-justice teaching" in Los Angeles, New York, Philadelphia, and other big cities.

The Social Justice High School in Chicago has a 100 percent Hispanic or black student body. The principal admits that the lessons taught there are often "atypical," such as teaching the relative likelihood of whites and minorities being pulled over by police.

Howard Zinn, the late author of the anti-American, but extremely popular, *People's History of the United States*, which is used as a history textbook in some schools, urges educators to prioritize "social justice" education over political neutrality. In a 1998 interview, he said his goal in writing *People's History* was to move us toward "democratic socialism" by a "quiet revolution." Zinn cites Germany, France, and Scandinavia for the United States to use as models.

This "social justice" curriculum results in a heavy cost in time not spent on the basics. Young Americans who are exposed to these radical left-wing ideas generally have no background information to help them evaluate biases and errors.

Sol Stern of the Manhattan Institute describes Education Professor William Ayers as one of the leaders in "bringing radical social-justice teaching into our public school classrooms." Most of Ayers's socialist propaganda is financed with taxpayers' money at state universities and teachers' colleges.

Ayers has taught that America is oppressive and unjust, that wealth and resources should be redistributed, and that only socialism can solve our problems. He speaks openly of his desire to use America's public school classrooms to train a generation of revolutionaries who will overturn the supposedly imperialistic regime of capitalist America.

From his prestigious and tenured university perch, Ayers for years has been teaching teachers and students rebellion against American capitalism and what he calls "imperialism" and "oppression." The code words for the Ayers curriculum are "social justice," a "transformative" vision, "critical pedagogy," "liberation," "capitalist injustices," "critical race theory," "queer theory," and of course multiculturalism and feminism.

That vocabulary is typical in the readings that Ayers assigns in his university courses. He admits he is a "communist street fighter" who has been influenced by Karl Marx, as well as by Che Guevara, Ho Chi Minh, and Malcolm X.

Ayers sees his education work as carrying on his radicalism in a new sphere. What he calls education "reform" focuses almost exclusively on teaching a "social justice" agenda in the classroom and a race-based approach to education policy. That's been his mission since he realized that revolution could be achieved more easily by teaching lies about America to public school students than by planting bombs.

Ayers wants teachers to be community organizers dedicated to provoking resistance to supposed racism and oppression. His education philosophy calls for infusing students and their parents with a radical political commitment, and downplaying achievement tests in favor of activism. His books are among the most widely used in America's 1,500 schools of education. Ayers even uses science and math courses as part of his "transformative" political strategy to teach that the American economic system is unjust.

Ayers teaches a course at the University of Illinois at Chicago called "On Urban Education," in which he calls for a "distribution of material and human resources." The course description states: "Homelessness, crime, racism, oppression—we have the resources and knowledge to fight and overcome these things. We need to look beyond our isolated situations, to define our problems globally. We cannot be child advocates...in Chicago or New York and ignore the web that links us with the children of India or Palestine." The readings he assigns for the course include Paolo Freire's *Pedagogy of the Oppressed*, two of Ayers's own books, and *Teaching to Transgress* by a radical black feminist.

Ayers maintains a busy lecture schedule at other schools of education and is a welcome visiting lecturer at Columbia Teachers College. He also does teacher training and professional development for Chicago public schools.

In a 2006 interview with *Revolution*, the magazine of the Marxist-Leninist-Maoist Revolutionary Communist Party, Ayers attacked American conservatives as "the most reactionary cabal of ideologues I've ever seen." Ayers complained that conservatives control "all three branches of the federal government, control many state governments, control the media—the kind of bought priesthood of the media that does nothing but bow down to them and kowtow to them."

QUEERING EDUCATION

Ayers endorsed a book called *Queering Elementary Education* by William J. Letts IV and James T. Sears, a collection of essays to teach adults and children to "think queerly." The blurb on the cover quotes Ayers as saying this is "a book for all teachers...and, yes, it has an agenda."

Ayers's far-out education theories have had a significant effect in education schools. One after another, teachers colleges are using their courses to promote socialist notions of wealth distribution, diversity, and environmentalism, and to punish students who resist this indoctrination by giving them low grades or even denying them graduation. The Department of Education lists fifteen high schools whose mission statements declare that their curricula center on "social justice."

Barack Obama claims that he knows William Ayers only as "a guy in the neighborhood." In fact, the unrepentant Ayers is a longtime friend and associate of Obama. Ayers and Obama worked closely together during the 1990s when Obama headed the Chicago Annenberg Challenge (CAC) and Ayers co-chaired the Chicago Annenberg Challenge's

Collaborative and also was ex officio a member of CAC's board. Obama served on the CAC board until 2001.

The CAC board made the fiscal decisions and the Collaborative set education policy. It's obvious that they had to have significant consultations about disbursement of the education grants. Obama was essentially authorizing the funding of education projects chosen by Ayers. The CAC gave $160 million in grants to so-called "school-reform" projects. Grant decisions initially put in place continued even after personnel changes.

Ayers was the founder and developer of a project known as the "small-schools" movement, a scheme that enabled Annenberg grants to be guided to "social justice"-themed schools built around specific political themes such as "inequity, war, and violence." The small-schools movement was heavily funded by CAC. CAC also funded teacher training to "teach against oppression" and America's alleged history of evil and racism.

According to Stanley Kurtz, senior fellow at the Ethics and Public Policy Center, a lot of CAC money was disbursed through so-called "external partners" with whom the small schools were required to affiliate, such as the Association of Community Organizations for Reform Now (ACORN). The Chicago Annenberg Challenge appears to be just another example of Republican foundation money—Walter Annenberg was President Richard Nixon's ambassador to Great Britain, a close friend and political supporter of Ronald Reagan, and an enormously generous philanthropist—taken over by leftists and used to advance left-wing causes. CAC's own final report on its education challenge compared the progress of students at schools that received Annenberg grants and schools that did not, concluding that "There were no statistically significant differences in student achievement between Annenberg schools and demographically similar non-Annenberg schools. This indicates that there was no Annenberg effect on achievement."

Obama authored two autobiographies but never wrote about his important executive experience in the 1990s with the Chicago Annenberg Challenge. Nor did he mention that his first candidacy for public office, when he ran for the Illinois State Senate, was launched at the home of William Ayers.

"Social justice" teaching is not only a terrible waste of precious school hours, it is grievously harmful to poor children. Sol Stern of the Manhattan Institute says, "Teaching for social justice is a cruel hoax on disadvantaged kids." It teaches grievance. It does not teach academic skills.

It also leads one to wonder what the federal Department of Education might do in a Barack Obama second term. Obama's Secretary of Education is Arne Duncan, who as Chicago School Superintendent worked with Obama back in the days when Obama was an associate of Bill Ayers and also had ties to the Chicago Annenberg Challenge. In the fall of 2008, when he was still Chicago School Superintendent, Duncan announced plans to open a "gay-friendly" public high school he first planned on calling "Pride Campus." The plan was for it to have 600 students, half homosexual and half heterosexual. Official materials proclaimed that the curriculum would "teach the history of all people who have been oppressed and the civil rights movements that have led to social justice and queer studies." After the announcement of Duncan's promotion, the opening of this unusual school was, as noted earlier, quietly blocked by the school board. But would a second Obama term lead to a federal program to seed such schools across the country? It's not hard to imagine.

It's no surprise that propaganda favoring Barack Obama is already finding favor with textbook publishers. The McDougal Littell 8th grade advanced English literature book (Houghton Mifflin Co., 2008) has fifteen pages featuring Barack Obama and his "life of service." A good way for parents to identify the bias of social studies textbooks is to check the index and then compare the coverage of Barack Obama and Ronald Reagan.

The Jesuits had a famous saying, "Give me a child for his first seven years, and I will give you the man." Obama has had the great good fortune of having his ideas taught in the public schools to children from kindergarten through twelfth grade, with the indoctrination revving up even further in college. "Social justice" is the secular substitute for Christian morality and ethics, and will be used in a second Obama term to further the advance of the state against free markets and the free exercise of religion.

CHAPTER ELEVEN

THE STATE AS PARENT

The Obama administration entertains a vision of American life very different from the way it has been lived in the past. In the past, Americans took pride in being faithful, hard-working, and self-sufficient. Obama wants to transfer the American people's faith in God to unquestioning faith in the state, and while he will still need hard-working people, self-sufficiency, for the 99 percent, should be passé. Obama's ambition for America is of cradle-to-grave government. It's no longer from ashes to ashes, from dust to dust, but from government-controlled hospitals, where one is born, to perhaps government-mandated rationing panels that would decide where and when one dies.

The Obama campaign has made this more or less explicit with its "The Life of Julia," a cartoon slide show about "how President Obama's policies [would] help one woman over her lifetime." The state gets its hands on Julia even before she starts kindergarten, when she's only three (children can never be separated from their parents and handed to the state too quickly), with a pre-K "Head Start" program. At seventeen she's the beneficiary of federal programs in high school (perhaps to be designed by Bill Ayers). Then, of course, the state sees her through college, helps with her loans, and keeps her, via Obamacare, a "child"—eligible to be covered by her parents' health insurance; and of course Obamacare guarantees her right to subsidized contraception and, should she "need" it, abortion. Once she "decides to have a child" (there is no sign that Julia ever gets married), the state stands ready to take care of everything. As a worker, the state, rather than the free market, determines her salary to make sure it is "equal" to that of her male compatriots and helps her eventually start her own business. Julia, apparently the single parent of a single child, then is dutifully grateful for all the federal programs that have turned public education into "social justice" education. Finally, she retires to get her due reward from the state, in the form of Medicare and Social Security.

Obama's America is one of state bankrolled radical individualism—of what's in it for me. It is the very same ideology that makes contraception a federally subsidized necessity and abortion a federally funded "choice." Obama also touts this vision as proving that he is a feminist, the candidate of women, as though the interests of women can be reduced to contraception and abortion, a limited if not degraded view of women's interests.

Unfortunately, as we know all too well, this radical individualist view has been advanced by the left through the courts and bureaucracies for decades. Just as the left has been busily remaking public education, they have been busily trying to undermine and redefine the family—not just through the highly visible push for gay marriage, but through divorce law and ideological feminism.

ANTI-FAMILY FEMINISTS

Among Obama's most vociferous supporters are militant feminists. And while Obama makes a pretense of championing faith and family, his feminist allies are among the most anti-family, anti-Christian groups active in politics. The most famous feminist political group, the National Organization for Women (NOW) supports all "abortion rights" including partial-birth abortion, gay and lesbian "rights," worldwide legalization of prostitution, and unrestricted access to pornography in libraries. According to an invaluable resource, the book *The Guide to Feminist Organizations* by Kimberly Schuld, "NOW revels in attacking Christianity and traditional values, conservative ideas and men," with Rush Limbaugh, conservative bishops, and evangelicals, among its favorite targets.

Most of the activist feminist organizations have non-profit status, many have interlocking boards of directors, and all of them have an interest in gaining money from left-wing foundations, corporations headed by weak-kneed executives, and grants of taxpayer funds (and they scoop up millions from each). Moreover, they are massively powerful in political fundraising—so much so that they have gained a stranglehold over the Democratic Party, making pro-life Democrats an endangered species.

The feminist groups pursue the same agenda, including government-funded daycare, paid entitlements for family leave, unrestricted access to abortion, "comparable worth," lesbian rights, affirmative action, and universal health insurance. Like all such left-wing groups, they are amazingly effective at penetrating and subverting mainstream organizations, in this case including the League of Women Voters and even the Girl Scouts who went feminist after they took Betty Friedan on their board; they dropped "loyalty" from the oath, began a condom-friendly sex-ed program, and made belief in God optional.

Again the thrust of all this is a radical individualism partnered with ever-increasing state power. Part and parcel of making belief in God optional is making parents optional. In Obama's war to displace religion with the state, it is important to displace a child's first (and primary) educators, parents, which is why the state is always pushing to enroll students, like Julia, at younger and younger ages, to extend the school day, and extend the school year. Another way to displace parents is through divorce, and we are perhaps only now seeing the results of what decades of easy divorce have done to a new generation of Americans who grew up without fathers. Government can be their sugar daddy.

The Judeo-Christian view, which has been the American view, is that the family is the fundamental institution of society, which is why it needs to be honored and protected. It is where children are raised. It is how society is built. It precedes the state and cannot justly be oppressed or displaced by the state. But radical leftists have long had a problem with the family, seeing it as a conservative, reactionary, patriarchal institution that can be a roadblock to state-driven "progressive reform" if parents are entitled to say "no."

Leftists know that when families are weak, the state can become strong, fulfilling roles that used to be filled by mothers and fathers. Radical feminists, for instance, knew that easy divorce, promoted as a means of liberating women, would cripple the traditional family. Radical feminists take it as a victory for women that family courts generally award sole or primary custody of most children of divorced parents to mothers, though the real effect of this is to make fathers irrelevant. "Julia," by the way, never appears to have any parents at all or, as noted, to show any signs of being married herself. She is a ward of the state and the state helps her raise her child.

In the past, Americans assumed that parents, not the state, could best determine what is in the best interests of their own children. For example, Chief Justice Warren Burger, writing in 1979 for the majority in *Parham* v. *J.R.*, stated that ever since Blackstone (who wrote in 1765), the law "has recognized that natural bonds of affection lead parents to act in the best interests of their children."

As recently as 2000, the Supreme Court in *Troxel* v. *Granville* reaffirmed this principle and upheld the "presumption that fit parents act in the best interests of their children." The *Troxel* case rejected the argument that a judge could supersede a fit parent's judgment about a child's "best interest."

But this has changed, and Obama appointees to the courts will make it change faster, taking away the rights of parents to say "no" to the state. Years ago, when Hillary Clinton proclaimed that it takes a village to raise a child, many people didn't realize that she was enunciating liberal dogma that the government should raise and control children. This concept fell on fertile soil when it reached activist judges eager to be anointed as elders of the child-raising village.

IT TAKES AN ACTIVIST COURT

Extremely instructive in the direction that Obama-appointed judges might take us is a ruling handed down by the U.S. Court of Appeals for the Ninth Circuit that was issued on November 2, 2005, and that we should examine in a little detail for its potential consequences for religious freedom, which, at bottom, is also a guarantee of parents' freedom against relentless coercion from the state. The court ruled that parents' fundamental right to control the upbringing of their children "does not extend beyond the threshold of the school door," and that a public school has the right to provide its students with "whatever information it wishes to provide, sexual or otherwise."

Instead of using the "village" metaphor, the judges substituted a Latin phrase that has the same effect. *Parens patriae* (the country as parent) was a legal concept used long ago by the English monarchy, but it never caught on in the United States, and the few mentions of it in U.S. cases are not relevant to this decision.

The Ninth Circuit case, *Fields* v. *Palmdale School District*, was brought by parents who discovered that their 7- to 10-year-old children had been required to fill out a nosy, 79-question survey about such matters as "thinking about having sex," "thinking about touching other people's private parts," and "wanting to kill myself." The decision claimed that the purpose of the psychological sex survey was "to improve students' ability to learn." That doesn't even pass the laugh test.

The parents were shocked and looked to the court for a remedy. No such luck. The three-judge Ninth Circuit panel unanimously ruled against the parents. One judge had been appointed by Jimmy Carter, one by Bill Clinton, and one by Lyndon B. Johnson. We live in times when judges (especially on the Left Coast) seize opportunities to create new law and new government powers even if they have to hide behind a Latin phrase of bygone years unknown to Americans.

The Ninth Circuit decision stated that "there is no fundamental right of parents to be the exclusive provider of information regarding sexual matters to their children" and that "parents have no due process or privacy right to override the determinations of public schools as to the information to which their children will be exposed."

The school had sent out a parental-consent letter, but it failed to reveal the intrusive questions about sex. The letter merely mentioned concerns about violence and verbal abuse, adding that if the child felt uncomfortable, the school would provide "a therapist for further psychological help." That should have been a warning, but many parents don't realize that the schools pursue an agenda unrelated to reading, writing, and 'rithmetic. Anticipating the new push to subject all school-children to mental health screening, the decision gratuitously stated that the school's power extends to "protecting the mental health of children."

The court didn't bother to defend the impertinent questionnaire itself, and said that public school authority is not limited to curriculum. The court made no mention of the need for informed parental consent or a right to opt out of an activity the parents deem morally objectionable.

The Ninth Circuit agreed with the lower court's broad ruling that the fundamental right to direct the upbringing and education of one's children does *not* encompass the right "to control the upbringing of their children by introducing them to matters of and relating to sex in accordance with their personal and religious values and beliefs."

How did the Ninth Circuit circumvent "the fundamental right of parents to make decisions concerning the care, custody, and control of their children," which has been U.S. settled law for decades? The court referred to this as the *Meyer-Pierce* right because it was first explicitly enunciated in two famous Supreme Court cases of the 1920s, *Meyer* v. *Nebraska* and *Pierce* v. *Society of Sisters*, and was reaffirmed as recently as 2000 in *Troxel* v. *Granville*.

The Ninth Circuit court said that since the government has put limits on parents' rights by requiring school attendance, therefore, the school can tell the students whatever it wants about sex, guns, the military, gay marriage, and the origins of life. The judges emphasized that once children are put in a public school, the parents' "fundamental right to control the education of their children is, at the least, substantially diminished."

How did the court feel empowered to put new limits on the settled law of *Meyer-Pierce* and give public schools the power to override parents on teaching about sex? Simple. The three liberal judges based their decision on "our evolving understanding of the nature of our Constitution."

Liberal judges have no shame in proclaiming their belief that our written Constitution is "evolving." In this case, the judges bragged that the Constitution has evolved to create the right to abortion, and then ruled that the evolving Constitution takes sex education away from parents and puts it "within the state's authority as *parens patriae*."

"The country as parent." That's Obama's view of our future.

CHAPTER TWELVE

OBAMA'S SECULARIZED JUDICIARY

Most people of faith recognize the American Civil Liberties Union (the ACLU) as one of their main legal opponents in disputes over freely expressing their religious beliefs. Liberal ACLU lawyers have long been a thorn in the side of religious Americans who think that schools should not be prayer-free zones, that public displays of the Ten Commandments are an expression of and not a violation of the First Amendment, and that crosses on public land should not be yanked out of the ground and broken up in the name of state-mandated secularism. What religious Americans might have been slow to realize is that the ACLU's long march through the institutions of America has culminated at the door of Obama's White House. Behind that door stands the one we have "been waiting for," as liberals chanted about Obama in 2008. Obama is the fulfillment of the ACLU's messianic secularist hopes.

No president has done more to empty the public square of Christians than Barack Obama. To the delight of secularists, Obama has been stacking the federal courts with ACLU-style judges who read the First Amendment through an ahistorical and atheistic prism, or as they like to call it, the "living Constitution," which is nothing more than a euphemism for whatever they think the Constitution *should* mean in our supposedly enlightened times.

David Hamilton is one of Obama's typical appointments to the court. Hamilton was nominated by the president for the Seventh Circuit Court of Appeals. He was Obama's first nominee to the courts. What was Hamilton's preparation for this august honor? Beyond his judicial experience, he had formerly worked in left-wing politics. In 1979, Hamilton worked for ACORN as a fundraiser in Philadelphia. In the late 1980s, David Hamilton served as vice president for litigation—and was a board member for—Indiana's ACLU branch.

A transparently ideological judge, Hamilton was even rated "not qualified" by the left-leaning American Bar Association. Hamilton was known for blocking pro-life and pro-decency laws. But he was most famous for his ACLU-style secularism.

In 2005, Hamilton struck down a prayer used in the Indiana legislature that mentioned Jesus Christ, ordering the Indiana House of Representatives to "refrain from using Christ's name or title or any other denominational appeal" and that such prayer "must be nonsectarian and must not be used to proselytize or advance any one faith or belief or to disparage any other faith or belief." Hamilton claimed that the "sectarian content of the substantial majority of official prayers in the Indiana House therefore takes the prayers outside the safe harbor the Supreme Court recognized for inclusive, non-sectarian legislative prayers in *Marsh* v. *Chambers*, 463 U.S. 783 (1983)."

At the same time, Hamilton instructed the Indiana legislature that the word "Allah" was permissible: "[t]he Arabic word 'Allah' is used for 'God' in Arabic translations of Jewish and Christian scriptures.... [i]f those offering prayers in the Indiana House of Representatives choose to use the Arabic Allah, the Spanish Dios, the German Gott, the French Dieu, the Swedish Gud, the Greek Theos, the Hebrew Elohim, the Italian Dio, or any other language's terms in addressing the God who is the focus of the non-sectarian prayers contemplated in *Marsh* v. *Chambers*, the court sees little risk that the choice of language would advance a particular religion or disparage others."

Public acknowledgment of Jesus Christ is unlawful; Islam's name for God isn't. So it goes in Obama's America—a far cry from the America of her second president, John Adams. "The experiment is made, and has completely succeeded: it can no longer be called in question, whether authority in magistrates, and obedience of citizens, can be grounded on reason, morality, and the Christian religion," he said. Adams had no qualms about calling America a Christian nation, with a Constitution designed for a people shaped by the Golden Rule and Ten Commandments: "Our constitution was made only for a moral and religious people. It is wholly inadequate for the government of any other."

The first Chief Justice of the Supreme Court, John Jay, also spoke of America as a Christian nation, writing to a clergyman in 1797: "Providence has given to our people the choice of their rulers, and it is the duty, as well as the privilege and interest of our Christian nation to select and prefer Christians for their rulers." Obama's judges consider America not a Christian but a publicly atheistic nation, which tolerates only the private expression of religion.

THE SIX COMMANDMENTS

Another defining ACLU-style judicial appointment by Obama was Virginia federal judge Michael Urbanski, who believes that in public settings the Ten Commandments should be reduced to the Six Commandments, sans the ones that mention God.

"Could the Ten Commandments be reduced to six, a federal judge asked Monday," reported the *Roanoke Times* in early May 2012. "That unorthodox suggestion was made by Judge Michael Urbanski during oral arguments over whether the display amounts to a governmental endorsement of religion, as alleged in a lawsuit filed by a student at Narrows High School."

"After raising many pointed questions about whether the commandments pass legal muster, the judge referred the case to mediation—with a suggestion: Remove the first four commandments, which are clearly religious in nature, and leave the remaining six, which make more secular commands, such as do not kill or steal," reported the paper.

"Ever since the lawsuit was filed in September amid heated community reaction, school officials have said the display is not religious because it also includes historical documents such as the Bill of Rights and the Declaration of Independence."

The *Roanoke Times* quotes Urbanski asking during a motions hearing in U.S. District Court in Roanoke: "If indeed this issue is not about God, why wouldn't it make sense for Giles County to say, 'Let's go back and just post the bottom six?'" He added, "But if it's really about God, then they wouldn't be willing to do that."

Urbanski then "directed attorneys on both sides to meet with Magistrate Judge Robert Ballou, who will lead mediation sessions," according to the paper. "If those discussions do not produce a settlement, Urbanski must decide whether the school board had religious intentions when it voted 3–2 last June to put the commandments back up after angry public reaction to their earlier removal."

Obama's secularized judges represent the consummation of a movement stretching back to the 1960s. Their decisions fulfill the hopes hatched in 1962 by secularists when the Supreme Court, for the first time ever, banned prayer in public schools. The landmark case was *Engel* v. *Vitale*, and the prayer at issue didn't even come close to entailing an establishment of religion. It wasn't even a sectarian prayer. It simply read: "Almighty God, we acknowledge our dependence upon Thee, and we beg Thy blessing upon us, our parents, our teachers and our Country."

At that moment, the national religion of secularism, for which Obama would one day serve as high priest, had been born. Far more dogmatic than any traditional religion, this federal religion of secularism crushes even the tiniest expressions of devotion to God in public life across the land.

Justice Potter Stewart dissented from his colleagues in *Engel* v. *Vitale*. He rebuked them for twisting the First Amendment into a cudgel of secularism: "The Court has misapplied a great constitutional principle. I cannot see how an 'official religion' is established by letting those who want to say a prayer say it. On the contrary, I think that to deny the wish of these school children to join in reciting this prayer is to deny them the opportunity of sharing in the spiritual heritage of our nation."

It is worth recalling that the Supreme Court's decision in *Engel* v. *Vitale* was severely and widely criticized at the time. Erwin Griswold, dean of the Harvard Law School, said that the court had no business even taking that case. In a major speech, he said that "it was unfortunate that the question involved in the Engel case was ever thought of as a matter for judicial decision." He added that "there are some matters which are essentially local in nature...to be worked out by the people themselves in their own communities."

Whether the justices realized it or not, the Court had just ratified the tyranny of the atheistic minority that would bedevil America for decades to come and that would set America's public schools on a course to becoming godless voids, with increasing doses of anti-Christian propaganda (under the guise of sex education) and ever-falling standards of decorum and achievement. Indeed, the beginning of public dissatisfaction with public schools can be traced to that very moment.

"In a country which has a great tradition of toleration, is it not important that minorities, who have benefited so greatly from that tolerance, should be tolerant, too?" asked Griswold. The intolerance of "tolerant" liberalism is a legacy of this ruling—a legacy that Obama personifies.

Obama has said that his judicial appointments must possess "empathy," but the religious receive no such "empathy" under his judicial supremacists. His judges only reserve empathy for the opponents of Judeo-Christian religious expression.

Obama's Six Commandments in Virginia, *pace* Urbanski, came in response to a complaint by the Freedom from Religion Foundation, a group of atheistic busybodies that seeks to banish Christians from the public square. Virginian parents were furious with the school board for at first pandering to this malicious group. Obama's judge, naturally, sided with the atheists. "It's clear to me that when the school board voted, there was only one thing on their mind. And that was God." Oh my! Urbanski ordered that the mediators determine whether the school board's vote was "secular" or was a response to "religious fervor." A better question might have been whether Urbanski believed that all historical documents mentioning God should be pruned of the word before exposing to the eyes of students.

A few of the lawyers before Urbanski were befuddled by his demand that they edit the Ten Commandments. One informed Urbanski that this request had never been made to him before. "Well, it's going to come up today," Urbanski replied.

Such is the caprice of Obama's judicial supremacists.

THE ACLU'S SCAVENGER HUNTS

The courtroom battles over the Ten Commandments began in 1980 with *Stone* v. *Graham*, when the Supreme Court ordered that framed copies of the Ten Commandments, which had been privately funded, be removed from Kentucky classrooms. That started a national campaign to remove the Ten Commandments from public buildings and parks all over the country. Most of these lawsuits were sparked by the ACLU or Americans United for Separation of Church and State.

In Utah, the ACLU even arranged a scavenger hunt offering a prize to anyone who could find another Ten Commandments monument that the ACLU could persuade an activist judge to remove. These monuments are worth a lot of money to the ACLU because federal law allows generous legal fees to be recovered for every Ten Commandments lawsuit the ACLU wins.

The most famous Ten Commandments case occurred in Montgomery, Alabama, where the ACLU sued to force removal of a Ten Commandments monument that had been installed in the colonnaded rotunda of the Alabama State Judicial Building on August 1, 2001, by Alabama Chief Justice Roy Moore. Shaped like a cube, this four-foot-tall monument displayed the Ten Commandments on the top. Each of the four sides of the cube featured famous American words: "Laws of nature and of nature's God" from the Declaration of Independence (1776), "In God We Trust" from our national motto (1956), "One nation under God, indivisible, with liberty and justice for all" from our Pledge of Allegiance (1954), and "So help me God" from the oath of office in the Judiciary Act (1789). The remaining space on the sides of the cube was filled with quotations from famous Americans such as George Washington, Thomas Jefferson, and John Jay, from British jurist William Blackstone, and from our National Anthem.

The ACLU filed suit to have the monument removed, and found a Carter-appointed federal judge willing to intervene in a state court matter. Myron H. Thompson was confirmed as a federal judge by the Democrat-controlled Senate in 1980 just a few months before the Reagan landslide.

Judge Thompson held a week-long trial, then ruled the Ten Commandments monument unconstitutional and ordered it removed from the State Judicial Building. It took him seventy-six pages to present his rationale in *Glassroth* v. *Moore* (2003). Thompson's principal holding was that "the Chief Justice's actions and intentions" violate the Establishment Clause of the First Amendment. Unable to demonstrate that the monument itself violated the First Amendment, Thompson rested his decision on Chief Justice Moore's speeches, writings, campaign literature, and associations.

Thompson personally went to view the monument and pronounced "the solemn ambience of the rotunda" and "sacred aura" about the monument as additional reasons why it was unconstitutional. He pretended to see the "sloping top" of the Ten Commandments tablets as unconstitutionally making the viewer think that they are an open Bible in disguise.

The "aura" about the monument was augmented, he said, by its location "in front of a large picture window with a waterfall in the background," so that you really can't miss seeing the monument. Thompson concluded that "a reasonable observer" would "feel as though the State of Alabama is advancing or endorsing, favoring or preferring, Christianity."

Thompson ordered the Ten Commandments removed because three attorney plaintiffs "consider the monument offensive. It makes them feel like outsiders."

But no atheist has any plausible claim to be offended by a reference to something he thinks does not exist. Atheists feign offense simply as a way to censor expressions of faith by others. In any case, the Founding Fathers did not write the Constitution to establish an atheistic tyranny of the minority.

That is Obama's goal, and his secularized judges are helping him to achieve it. In 2011, Obama succeeded in appointing another secular-activist lawyer to a lifetime position on the federal bench—Edward Chen, who worked as a pro-abortion ACLU lawyer in San Francisco for sixteen years.

The ACLU is to Obama's judiciary what the minor leagues are to the majors.

"I think we're seeing a common DNA run through the Obama nominees, and that's the ACLU chromosome," said Senator Jeff Sessions of Alabama after the president nominated Chen.

Around the time that the HHS mandate was announced, Obama succeeded in elevating yet another opponent of religious freedom to the federal courts—Jesse M. Furman, whose brother works for Obama as an economic adviser. Oklahoma Senator Jim Inhofe and thirty-three other senators objected to Furman's nomination to the U.S. District Court for the Southern District of New York.

"In keeping with President Obama's attack on religious freedom related to the contraception ruling, this nomination further shows President Obama's disregard for religious liberty in America," said Inhofe. "Here we have an Obama appointee who in essence sought to keep religion and religious view points out of the public square. His position was both an assault on the free exercise of religion and an attack on free speech. In short, Furman encouraged judicial activism against religious expression, because he apparently finds the message of Christianity offensive."

Furman, as a lawyer in private practice, had supported the Anti-Defamation League and other groups in the *Good News Club* v. *Milford Central School* case. The case involved a public elementary school which blocked an evangelical Christian club for children from using the school facilities for its meetings outside school hours. Furman argued that the school was right to box out the evangelical Christian club. "While the public school is designed to promote cohesion among a heterogeneous democratic people, the Good News Club is designed to do quite the opposite: to label people as 'saved' or 'unsaved' and, thus, to promote religious belief in general and Christian belief in particular," argued Furman.

Furman's case lost before the Supreme Court. In a 6–3 opinion, the Supreme Court disagreed with Furman and the elementary school, arguing that the public elementary school had no right to police viewpoints within a "limited public forum."

Obama's judges share his contempt for the original meaning of the Constitution. He has long seen the U.S. Constitution as an obstacle to what he considers progress. In a 2001 interview that surfaced during the 2008 presidential campaign, he made this very clear: the Supreme Court under Justice Earl Warren had failed to break "free from the essential constraints that were placed by the Founding Fathers in the Constitution," Obama told the host of a radio show.

The Warren Court was insufficiently radical, he said. It conceded too much ground to the traditional interpreters of the Constitution as a "charter of negative liberties," which "says what the states can't do to you, says what the federal government can't do to you, but doesn't say what the federal government or state government must do on your behalf."

The Founding Fathers, he implied, had written a defective document, much too passive in its understanding of the federal government's possibilities. The Founders had set up a form of government to protect liberty; he clearly wished they had formed a government to enact equality.

The arrogance of his presidency derives in large part from this view. Obama measures progress not by adherence to the Constitution but by infidelity to it. He wants not a "charter of negative liberties," but a Leviathan, which he calls a "living" Constitution, that swallows them up in the pursuit of egalitarianism and libertinism.

What "makes us the United States of America," Obama has said, is the "scale" of government's ambitions. No, what "makes us the United States of America" is preservation of the Constitution.

America has entered into a new and glorious phase, according to Obama, where no one should quibble over such antiquated matters as constitutional limitation or the Founders' meaning of the Establishment clause.

In that 2001 interview, Obama said he was "not optimistic about bringing major redistributive change through the courts." But now he is. His judges uphold his "living" Constitution at every turn. Of course, his "living" Constitution means the real one is dead in practice. The question before voters in 2012 is: Will Americans go back to living under the actual Constitution or continue to succumb to Obama's fake one that is swallowing up our freedoms? What Obama has dismissively described as outmoded "constraints that were placed by the Founding Fathers in the Constitution" look very sensible after four years of his willful statism.

CHAPTER THIRTEEN

OBAMA'S SECULARIST CZARS

In addition to stacking the courts with secularists, Obama has also been smuggling them into key government agencies as "czars." Many of these secularists come armed with stunningly amoral plans—schemes that even exceed the morbid imagination of Aldous Huxley in his novel *Brave New World*.

Obama's so-called "Regulatory Czar" (Administrator of the White House Office of Information and Regulatory Affairs), Cass Sunstein, wrote a book in 2008 in which he declared that the government "owns the rights to body parts of people who are dead or in certain hopeless conditions, and it can remove their organs without asking anyone's permission." What Sunstein envisioned is coming to pass, thanks to Obama's HHS.

In 2010, officials at HHS acknowledged that it was pushing the grotesque practice of harvesting organs from urgent-care patients in emergency rooms. According to the *Washington Post*, taxpayers have been financing, via a $321,000 HHS grant, a pilot program at the University of Pittsburgh Medical Center-Presbyterian Hospital and Allegheny General Hospital in Pittsburgh to obtain organs from emergency room patients, a practice heretofore "considered off-limits in the United States because of ethical and logistical concerns."

The goal of the pilot project, reported the *Washington Post*, is to "investigate whether it is feasible and, if so, to encourage other hospitals nationwide to follow."

Usually liberal on social issues, the *Washington Post* seemed to pause on this one, acknowledging in its story that bringing transplant teams into emergency rooms marked a possibly disturbing new milestone for society: "Critics say the program represents a troubling attempt to bring a questionable form of organ procurement into an even more ethically dicey situation: the tumultuous environment of an ER, where more than ever it raises the specter of doctors preying on dying patients for their organs."

Many liberal-leaning bioethicists find this practice unseemly. "There's a fine line between methods that are pioneering and methods that are predatory," the *Post* quoted bioethicist Leslie M. Whetstine. "This seems to be in the latter category. It's ghoulish."

Their fear is that doctors will increasingly give patients less care, seeing them as organ donors rather than patients, and in the haste of removing the organs, transplant teams won't bother to investigate "consent" too carefully. (Did the person really give "informed" consent? Or did they just superficially sign off on a driver's license designation?)

"Imagine you have a 20-year-old inner-city kid who gets shot. Twenty minutes later, a family member comes in and says, 'What happened?' They're told, 'We tried to save him but couldn't, and he had an organ donor card so we took an organ,'" the *Post* quoted University of Pennsylvania bioethicist Arthur Caplan. "You can imagine they're going to think, 'Did you really do everything you could to save him?'"

Bioethicist Michael Grodin was quoted as saying of the practice: "When you do this stuff in such close proximity to treating the patient, the people in the emergency room will quickly start to think, 'This is a potential organ donor' even when they are treating the patient.... People are going to wonder, if they are being treated in the ER, 'Are the transplant people going to swoop down to get my organs?'"

Nevertheless, Obama has proceeded in his promotion of the practice, and that's not his only grim accomplishment in this harvesting field. According to the *Post*, he "restarted" a "federally funded DCD [Donation after Cardiac Death] pilot project" in Colorado that takes "hearts from babies 75 seconds after" they are taken off life support.

GREEN ABORTIONS

Obama made John Holdren, another proponent of the Brave New World, his "science czar" (Director of the White House Office of Science and Technology Policy). Holdren has written in support of so-called green abortions. "Compulsory control of family size is an unpalatable idea, but the alternatives may be much more horrifying," Holdren has written. According to a textbook Holdren co-authored, involuntary birth control measures, including forced sterilization, make sense given "climate change" and the famine it could cause. Holdren's textbook was called *Ecoscience: Population, Resources, Environment*, and had as its co-authors the discredited population control alarmist Paul R. Ehrlich and his wife Anne.

"When performed today under appropriate medical circumstances by a qualified physician...abortion is much safer than a full-term pregnancy," Holdren and the Ehrlichs wrote, recommending the practice as a form of survival on a wobbly planet.

"An abortion is clearly preferable to adding one more child to an overburdened family or an overburdened society, where the chances that it will realize its potential are slight," Holdren and the Erhlichs wrote in the 1977 edition of *Ecoscience*.

"There is little question that legalized abortion can contribute to a reduction in birth rates," the authors continued. "Liberalization of abortion policies in those countries where it is still largely or entirely illegal is therefore justifiable both on humanitarian and health grounds and as an aid to population control."

In 1969, Holdren wrote that "if the population control measures are not initiated immediately, and effectively, all the technology man can bring to bear will not fend off the misery to come." For those who care about religious freedom—or freedom full stop—the ideas of this Malthusian science czar should be troubling. Clearly, the mandates behind Obamacare could easily, with men like these providing the rationale, expand into ever more extreme measures. It is never prudent to hand one's body, or one's conscience, to the state.

Obama has shown that his preferred manner of administration is through unaccountable czars, many of them familiar with Chicago-style politics, such as Obama's "food czar," Sam Kass. Officially, he is labeled Senior Policy Adviser for Healthy Food Initiatives, but he's joining the list of more than thirty-five czars given broad and unaccountable power over our lives, habits, and spending.

Everybody laughed when Senator Tom Coburn of Oklahoma asked Supreme Court nominee Elena Kagan if it would be constitutional for Congress to order Americans "to eat three vegetables and three fruits every day." Kagan declined to give a straightforward answer, maybe because she knew that exactly that type of dictatorial mandate is coming soon, in both Obamacare and a ukase issued by the food czar.

Even scarier than Kass is Obama's health czar, Donald Berwick, who is the top administrator over Medicare and Medicaid. The life-and-death powers he exercises, the huge sums of taxpayer money he directs, and the dishonest way Obama evaded the Senate's constitutional right to interrogate and reject him, make Berwick arguably the most shocking of all Obama's appointments.

Obama told Joe the Plumber that he wanted to redistribute the wealth. We didn't realize what else Obama planned to redistribute. Czar Berwick is on record as saying, "Excellent health care is by definition redistributional." He used this favorite Obama term in the context of praising Britain's socialized medicine system as "a global treasure" and said, "I love it."

Around the time of Obama's announcement of Berwick's appointment, one of Britain's leading conservative newspapers, the *Sunday Telegraph*, uncovered widespread cuts in British health care that were adopted in secret and buried in obscure appendices and lengthy policy documents. These include restrictions on common operations such as hip and knee replacements and cataract surgery, the closure of many nursing homes for the elderly, and a reduction in hospital beds and staff.

Berwick admits that redistributing health care means rationing health care, which is why he has been called a one-man death panel. He has admitted in an interview, "The decision is not whether or not we will ration care—the decision is whether we will ration with our eyes open."

Note the imperial "we." That's the way czars talk.

Like a quintessential totalitarian socialist, Berwick assumes that smart bureaucrats should make life-and-death decisions and spend the money belonging to those they disdain as dumb, ordinary citizens. Berwick said, "I cannot believe that the individual health care consumer can enforce through choice the proper configurations of a system as massive and complex as health care. That is for leaders to do."

Berwick even promises he will train young doctors and nurses to understand "the risks of too great an emphasis on individual autonomy." To eliminate individual health care choices, Berwick's bureaucracy will have a budget that is larger than the Defense Department and is 4 percent of our GDP. Czars with such power will likely give short shrift to the moral and ethical concerns of Christian doctors and patients. Their Christian "prejudices" (or principles) will be judged irrational, in a bureaucratic sense, and their "individual autonomy" is unlikely to be respected in the vast bureaucrat-managed machine that is socialized medicine.

Berwick's paper trail of "baggage" is why Obama gave him a recess appointment. He wanted to avoid the Senate's advice-and-consent power altogether and keep Berwick's damaging statements out of the news. But in appointing him a czar, Obama—apparently—was not troubled by Berwick's extremism at all.

The term "czar" has come to mean a presidential crony appointee who was never vetted by the Senate and who exercises sweeping regulatory authority without congressional oversight. Obama has done more czar-crowning than any other administration by far; and the bureaucratic initiatives of the czars are on top of the vastly increased regulations issued by other already established agencies.

It goes without saying that the Founding Fathers believed in limited government. It also used to be understood that one of the social benefits of a Christian people is that they were self-governing. In the American experience, this meant that in acting out their Christian lives in the public and private spheres, they tried to be honest and generous and upstanding and self-reliant; they were not in need of continual government intervention, nannying, or control.

But in the secular Obama world, government guides everything, because government knows best. Consider that Obamacare's 2,000-plus pages created about 160 new agencies and boards with regulatory power. The Department of Health and Human Services published 864 pages of regulations to govern electronic medical records.

President Obama signed the 2,300-page Dodd-Frank financial reform bill. Its implementation required at least 243 new regulations by 11 federal agencies, several of which did not yet exist at the time of passage.

Obama's secretary of Energy, Steven Chu, bragged that under his leadership, the Department of Energy (DOE) has "accelerated the pace" of regulation and "placed new resources and emphasis behind the enforcement" of new regulations, which "increase the stringency" of "minimum conservation standards" for all sorts of home appliances. It is not the "religious right" that has sent policemen into bedrooms, it is the bureaucratic left, whose energy police will ensure that your thermostat is set properly and you are using the right sort of light bulbs (and the secret police of the science czar might be there as well with a mandatory, Obamcare-insurance-covered condom-dispensing machine). The DOE will even regulate that cozy bedroom fireplace you had installed. The department has issued a new rule that gas fireplace logs cannot use more than 9,000 BTUs per hour, which is about one-tenth of what current gas logs require. This new rule will wipe out the gas fireplace industry, and the gas logs in our homes would become illegal.

Obama wasn't kidding when he promised to "fundamentally transform the United States." He has figured out how to bypass Congress and rule us by czars and a rod of regulations.

THE FEMINIST CZAR

Naturally, Obama has pandered to the secularized feminists with their own czar. He pushed through legislation that created a czar over women's issues worldwide. Based in the State Department, her statutory title is "Ambassador-at-Large for Global Women's Issues." Her task is to assure a "gender integration" perspective in all State Department policies and programs. The breathtaking reach of her powers is openly stated in the first section of the bill which created the job: "The Ambassador shall coordinate and advise, and where relevant lead—(1) State Department activities and policies, including as they affect programs and funding relating to prevention and response, including gender integration and women's development internationally as relates to prevention and response." And if that's not enough, the feminist ambassador is also responsible for the "allocation of State Department resources" to carry out the mischief.

One important vehicle for spending these taxpayer dollars is the International Violence Against Women Act, which assures that the feminist left controls the flow of taxpayers' money. Section 112 provides for grants to "Women's Nongovernmental Organizations and Community-Based Organizations." It's a no-brainer to predict what kinds of "organizations" will be eligible for those grants. You can be sure that non-feminist organizations will not be on any approved list of grantees. In fact, the entire purpose of the feminist czar is to act as an international missionary for the feminist movement. The Obama administration would surely find it unthinkable for the government to fund sending Christian missionaries abroad, but doesn't bat an eyelash at subsidizing global feminism, with its own secular ideology and very limited view of "women's issues."

For instance, does anyone think that the State Department will call for stopping the violence against women that comes from mandatory abortions carried out to support a government's one-child policy? Or report on sex-selective abortions to kill unborn girl babies because parents prefer a boy baby? If our State Department wants to help women in other countries, how about reporting to the American people on the atrocities against women committed by Muslim countries that use sharia law? That includes forced marriages, child marriages, so-called "honor" murders, polygamy, and death by stoning as punishment for women who commit adultery.

The State Department could do something very useful by refusing to grant visas or immigrant status to anyone who supports sharia punishments or genital mutilation of women. That would be an inexpensive way to stop a lot of violence against women. But in Obamaworld, we are not allowed to make cultural judgments against Islam, and we are not allowed to impose views that might be labeled "Christian"—such as respect for

life, the family's independence from the state, and the dignity of women—
on others. But we can still spend millions of taxpayer dollars for a radical
feminist group in India, Women Power Connect, to lobby for more
Indian women parliamentarians, or to push Kenyans to put abortion
rights into their constitution, or to subsidize myriad other bureaucratic
feminist initiatives.

Obama's czar over women's issues is Melanne Verveer, who was Hillary Clinton's chief of staff in the Bill Clinton White House. Verveer was
also executive vice president for the People for the American Way, a left-
wing lobbying group founded in direct opposition to the so-called religious right, where she played a key role in destroying Robert Bork's
nomination to the Supreme Court. A graduate of Georgetown University,
Verveer once worked at the United States Conference of Catholic bishops,
supporting the efforts of the Catholic left.

When liberals say that conservatives exaggerate the radicalism of the
Obama administration, conservatives might ask in turn why Obama
needs so many unaccountable czars at his beck and call; why his administration enacts so many shadowy regulations to bind us all; and just what
limits the Obama administration—and its radical ideologue czars—
might respect when it comes to our freedoms, especially our freedoms
guaranteed under the First Amendment, particularly in light of the
administration's relentlessly secularist anti-Christian policies at home
and abroad.

CHAPTER FOURTEEN

CIVIL DISOBEDIENCE IN OBAMA'S SECOND TERM

O bama's assault on the religious freedom of Americans raises the very real prospect of civil disobedience.

In the fifth century, St. Augustine posed a powerful rhetorical question to Christians: "What does it really matter to a man whose days are numbered what government he must obey, so long as he is not compelled to act against God or his conscience?" St. Augustine accepted that Christians must render unto Caesar what is Caesar's, but not if Caesar is determined to usurp the role of God.

St. Thomas Aquinas also made this argument powerfully in the *Summa Theologica*. He held that an unjust law is no law. Martin Luther King Jr. referenced the thought of both St. Augustine and St. Thomas Aquinas in his famous "Letter from Birmingham Jail."

America's Founding Fathers, as men of deep learning and culture, were steeped in this Christian intellectual tradition and used it to justify their breaking away from the tyranny of King George III. Civil disobedience is as American as apple pie.

Obama doesn't seem to realize that he is sawing off the branch on which he sits. If he can disobey the supreme law of the land, why can't the people disobey his laws? Egotistical pols and activist judges who now live by lawlessness will one day die by it. By rejecting the law and putting in its place their own personal opinions, they invite the people to imitate them and disregard their decrees with the same willfulness with which they disregard the Constitution. If Obama isn't bound by the Framers' words, why are the people bound by his?

The tree of liberty is fertilized by the blood of tyrants, said Thomas Jefferson. What would Jefferson say today? Next to the growing tyranny of Obama, the grievances Jefferson enumerated against the British crown in the Declaration of Independence look almost minor. King George III, for all of his injustices, never forced the colonists to submit to the false gods of secularism.

"No provision in our Constitution ought to be dearer to man than that which protects the rights of conscience against the enterprises of the civil authority," wrote Thomas Jefferson. The manifest purpose of the Framers' First Amendment was not freedom from religion but freedom for religion.

Pandering to a largely Muslim audience in Turkey in 2009, Obama said that "we do not consider ourselves a Christian nation." The Founding Fathers did. They taught their children to look with respect upon the first explorers and colonists who had dedicated this continent to the triune God.

"It was the Lord who put into my mind the fact that it would be possible to sail to the Indies.... [The] inspiration [came] from the Holy Spirit, because he comforted me with rays of marvelous inspiration from the Holy Scriptures," wrote Christopher Columbus.

In 1607, when the first English settlers landed in Jamestown, Virginia, they immediately planted a cross and claimed the land for Jesus Christ.

William Bradford, governor of the Plymouth colony, wrote that the mission of the Pilgrims was to "advance the gospel and kingdom of Christ in the remote parts of the world." The Pilgrims signed a document that came to be known as the Mayflower Compact. It was an agreement made not with each other but with God Almighty. The document began with the words, "In the name of God, Amen."

Out of this ethos of respect for religion came such acts of the first Congress as the Northwest Ordinance. Enacted by Congress in 1789, it required that all schools be instituted for the purpose of teaching religion, stating: "Religion, morality, and knowledge, being necessary to good government and the happiness of mankind, schools and the means of education shall forever be encouraged."

George Washington's famous Farewell Address warned future generations of Americans never to forget that the United States cannot endure without the "indispensable supports" of morality and religion. Even the cranky, sometimes skeptical Benjamin Franklin allowed at the Constitutional Convention: "I have lived long, sir, and the longer I live the more convincing proofs I see of this truth—that God governs in the affairs of men."

RELIGION, THE FOUNDATION OF A FREE SOCIETY

To our nation's Founders, freedom of religion was a nonnegotiable condition for the survival of a free society. Trampling on the conscience rights of the religious as Obama has done would have been unthinkable to them. James Madison, hailed as the Father of the Constitution, described conscience as "the most sacred of all property." He stressed that "the Religion then of every man must be left to the conviction and conscience of every man; and it is the right of every man to exercise it as these may dictate."

"The establishment of civil and religious Liberty was the motive that induced me to the field of battle," said America's first president, George Washington.

In 1803, Thomas Jefferson reassured the Ursuline Sisters—who had been running schools, orphanages, and hospitals in French-controlled Louisiana since their arrival in 1727—that the principles of the Constitution were a "sure guarantee" of their religious freedom. Your ministry, Jefferson told the sisters, could "govern itself according to its own voluntary rules, without interference from the civil authority."

This extraordinary exchange of letters between the New Orleans Ursuline Sisters and Jefferson is worth reproducing in full, as it bears directly upon Catholic fears of Obama today. Keep in mind as you read the letters that the Ursuline Sisters came from France and possessed fresh information, received through letters from their persecuted confreres in Europe, about the secularist heel under which the French Revolutionaries kept the Church there.

Historians record that the New Orleans Ursulines knew all about the French National Assembly's laws forbidding nuns from wearing their habits. They knew all about the French Revolutionaries' confiscation of monastic property and convents. They knew of the Diderot-style secularists who were clamoring for Christianity to be buried in the ash heap of history and to be replaced by the "Goddess of Reason." They knew of the exiled priests and imprisoned nuns who refused to swear oaths of allegiance to the French Revolutionaries. They knew of fellow Ursulines who had been guillotined for operating an "illegal" school.

And so these shrewd and courageous nuns—who now found themselves, after the Louisiana Purchase, under American authority—wrote to Jefferson and demanded in effect a reassurance from him of their religious liberty:

To Thomas Jefferson, President of the United States of America
    Dear Sir:

The Ursuline Religious of New Orleans, encouraged by the honorable mention which you so kindly made of their order, take the liberty of having recourse to you in regard to some business which is of great concern to their Institute.

Although no express mention has been made of it, they think that the Treaty of Cession and still more the spirit of justice which characterizes the United States of America, will certainly guarantee to those seeking your help the continued enjoyment of their present property. But, keeping to them, they believe that they would certainly fail in one of their principal obligations were they to neglect to see to it that this right of their property be put officially in writing, confirming their rights to this property not only for themselves but also for those of their Sisters who will succeed them; and, for this reason, to beg you, dear sir, to present our petition to the congress in the manner and form which you will judge the most suitable.

This request of the Ursulines of New Orleans is not dictated by personal interest nor ambitious aims. Separated from the world and its pomps and vanities, and, in a word, from all that is called its advantages, they have scarcely any ambition for earthly goods; but, bound by the solemn vow to use their time in the formation of youth, they cannot help but be anxious to know if they will be able with certainty to count on the continued enjoyment of their revenues which will enable them to fulfill their obligations. It is, then, less their own interests which they plead than it is that of the public good. In reality, it is the cause of the orphan and the abandoned child, of unfortunates brought up in the midst of the horrors of vice and infamy who come to be reared by us in the ways of Religion and virtue, and be given a formation which will enable them one day to become happy and useful citizens. Finally, it is in the interest of this country which can but reap for itself honor and glory in encouraging and protecting an establishment as useful, and, we might even say, as necessary as ours. Dear sir, we who seek your help dare to believe that these considerations will make an impression on you. Even more, we dare to count in advance on your protection.

With the most profound respect, "Monsieur le President," we have the honor of being

Your very humble and very obedient servants

The Ursulines of New Orleans
Sr. Marie Therese Farjon of St. Xavier Superior

March 21, 1804
Washington, May 15, 1804
To the Soeur Therese de St. Xavier Farjon Superior and the nuns of the order of St. Ursula at New Orleans

I have received, holy sisters, the letter you have written me wherein you express anxiety for the property vested in your institution by the former governments of Louisiana. The principles of the constitution and government of the United States are a guarantee to you that it will be preserved to you, sacred and inviolate, and that your institution will be permitted to govern itself according to its own voluntary rules, without interference from the civil authority. Whatever diversity of shade may appear in the religious opinions of our fellow citizens, the charitable objects of your institution cannot be indifferent to any; and its furtherance of the wholesome pur-poses of society, by training up its younger members in the way they should go, cannot fail to ensure it the patronage of the government it is under [the government of the Louisiana terri-tory]. Be assured it will meet all the protection which my office can give it. I salute you, holy sisters, with friendship & respect.

Thomas Jefferson

JAIL FOR THE RESISTANT RELIGIOUS?

Could anyone imagine Barack Obama or Kathleen Sebelius writing such a letter to the Ursulines today? No, their "living Constitution" permits them to violate the religious freedom of nuns and priests and Catholic doctors and nurses who perform corporal works of mercy. If they wish to help the poor in the public square, they must first bow to Obama's secularism. And if they don't, Obama can fine them $2,000 per employee (and then liquidate their property and imprison their institutions' officers if they refuse).

Obama's abuse of religious freedom justifies vigorous civil disobedi-ence. Should Obama capture a second term, a dramatic showdown will occur and should occur. Given that much of the judiciary is in his pocket and Congress lacks the will to stop him, nothing else could smash his secularist monopoly than widespread civil disobedience.

What would Obama do if millions of Catholics, Jews, and evangeli-cals banded together to practice civil disobedience against the HHS mandate? The costs of civil disobedience are high if few practice it. But if many do, those costs drop, and even tyrants can grow scared. Would widespread civil disobedience shock Obama enough to sign a law from

Congress rescinding the HHS order? Or, enjoying the safety of a second term, would he dig in and fight?

In March 2012, Obama, not realizing that he was speaking into an open microphone, whispered to Russian President Dmitri Medvedev, "This is my last election. After my election I have more flexibility." It is a chilling comment. What new radicalism awaits Americans?

In February 2012, congressional Republicans held a hearing on Obama's HHS mandate and asked religious leaders a simple question: Would you go to jail rather than comply with this decree?

"We're not going to violate our consciences," William E. Lori, now the Roman Catholic bishop of Baltimore, said to Congressman Trey Gowdy. The Reverend Dr. Matthew C. Harrison, president of the Lutheran Church's Missouri Synod, said, "Yes, I would, clearly [go to jail]." Dr. Ben Mitchell, a philosophy professor at Union University, echoed Dr. Harrison's sentiments.

"Well, just so everybody understands what is going to happen: These guys are either going to go to jail because they won't violate their religious beliefs, or the hospitals and the schools are going to close, which means government is going to get bigger, because they're going to have to fill the void that is left when you guys quit doing it," said Congressman Gowdy. "And maybe that's what they wanted all along."

Evangelical pastor Rick Warren, who delivered the invocation at Obama's inauguration, tweeted, "I'm not a Catholic but I stand in 100% solidarity with my brothers & sisters to practice their belief against govt pressure," adding, "I'd go to jail rather than cave in to a government mandate that violates what God commands us to do. Would you? Acts 5:29."

Protestant leader Richard Land sounded ready to go to jail too:

> The Obama administration's brazen determination to force
> all Americans to pay for abortions is an affront to our

nation's core commitment to liberty of conscience. A person who is not free to follow the dictates of his or her moral conscience is not free. Government has no authority to dictate compliance on matters that do such violence to the consciences of a vast segment of the population. The Obama administration has declared war on religion and freedom of conscience. This must not stand. Our Baptist forebears died and went to prison to secure these freedoms. It is now our calling to stand in the gap and defend our priceless First Amendment religious freedoms.

Obama is on a collision course with the religious. Is he prepared in his second term to throw priests, pastors, and rabbis into prison?

CHAPTER FIFTEEN

THE CULT
OF OBAMA

If you send your children to a public school, they may have already been indoctrinated in the cult of Obama-worship. Under Obama's secularism, the state assumes the place of God. Hence, it shouldn't surprise us that Obama worship has taken place in America's public schools.

The "I pledge" video, in which celebrities touted Obama's policies, shown in Utah in August 2009, was not isolated evidence of indoctrination of public schoolchildren in the new cult of Obama-worship. Also in 2009, second-graders in New Jersey were taught to sing songs of praise and fidelity to Barack Obama in February and again in June, and parents only found out about it in September.

Public schoolchildren are now forbidden to sing Christmas carols that mention the real meaning of Christmas (only songs like "Rudolph the Red-Nosed Reindeer" are allowed), but in New Jersey, second-graders were taught to sing the spiritual "Jesus Loves the Little Children" in which Jesus' name was replaced with Obama's. They sang,

He said red, yellow, black, or white
All are equal in his sight
Barack Hussein Obama.

Before Obama's election, it was considered a political no-no for
Republicans to use his middle name. Beginning with his inauguration
in January 2009, he and his followers started using Hussein to glorify his
Muslim heritage and connections.

The revised lyrics taught the kids that Obama will "make this country strong again." The lyrics promote Obama's "Lilly Ledbetter law" by
including the line:

He said we must be fair today
Equal work means equal pay.

New Jersey second-graders were taught to sing a second Obama-
personality-cult song to the tune of the "Battle Hymn of the Republic."
Here are some of the lyrics:

Mr. President, we honor you today!
For all your great accomplishments, we all doth say "hooray."
Hooray, Mr. President! You're number one!
Hooray, Mr. President, we're really proud of you!
So continue, Mr. President, we know you'll do the trick
So here's a hearty hip hooray, Hip, hip hooray!

These songs were not spontaneous kiddie exuberance or extracur-
ricular playground activity. The video makes clear that the teacher was
methodically instructing the children, using one talented second-grader
to demonstrate exactly how to sing the songs, and coaching students who
forgot the words.

The teacher also led the children in giving a sort of Heil Obama salute. On cue, they outstretched their right hands, accentuating their community of action in praising Obama. A poster for the book *I Am Barack Obama* by activist Charisse Carney-Nunes could be seen near the chanting second-graders.

The New Jersey songs were first taught to the children at B. Bernice Young Elementary School in February to celebrate Black History Month, and then videotaped in June as part of a Father's Day tribute to Barack Obama. Only after the video was later posted on the internet did parents learn about it.

Who's responsible for this outrage? The teacher has retired with full pension and benefits. The principal, Dr. Denise King, defended the controversial song, making no apologies. Parents quoted the principal as saying she would allow the performance again if she could. King touted her trip to Obama's inauguration in the school yearbook along with Obama campaign slogans and pictures she took in Washington on January 20, and she has posted pictures of Obama in the school's hallways.

Superintendent Christopher Manno issued a written statement that the taping and its distribution were unauthorized, but failed to say whether the singing lesson was approved. State Education Commissioner Lucille Davy directed the superintendent to review this matter but declined to say what the review will cover or if any action would be taken.

Some shocked comments from parents included: "I can't believe it's our school. We don't want to praise this guy like he's a god or an idol or a king." "I felt this was reminiscent of 1930s Germany, and the indoctrination of children to worship their leader." Former RNC chair Michael Steele said: "This is the type of propaganda you would see in Stalin's Russia or Kim Jong-il's North Korea."

A significant part of Barack Obama's plan to "change" America involves having the federal government take control of public school curricula, plus compiling a database of personal information about each student. The takeover is planned to be accomplished by attaching extraordinary strings to the $128 billion of "Stimulus" funds shoveled into education.

On September 8, 2009, Obama gave a speech broadcast to every schoolchild in America, which kicked up a storm of controversy. A study plan for his speech produced by the U.S. Department of Education, not hiding its political motives, was sent out to schools in advance.

The politics of Obama's extraordinary internet visit to all classrooms was presaged by the August 28 showing of the "I pledge" video at an assembly of the Eagle Bay Elementary School in Farmington, Utah. This four-minute video calls on viewers to pledge "to be a servant to our President" and pledge "to be of service to Barack Obama."

This video presents about fifty celebrity-type persons saying, "I pledge…" to take some left-wing action, such as supporting federal health care legislation, advancing stem-cell research, working for UNICEF, or signing up with Serve.gov to do community service.

Many of the "I pledge" statements support goals of the left-wing environmentalists, such as pledging "to sell my obnoxious car and buy a hybrid," to reduce use of plastics, to buy less bottled water, not to use plastic bags at the grocery store, and not to flush a toilet after only urinating. One pledge parodies our traditional Pledge of Allegiance: "I pledge allegiance to the funk, to the united funk of funkadelica."

After vigorous criticism from parents, the Utah principal apologized for showing this video, but the children had already been propagandized to support Barack Obama.

STATE-SANCTIONED BRAINWASHING

Before Obama's September 8 speech to all schoolchildren, Secretary of Education Arne Duncan sent instructions to all school principals urging them to use this "historic moment" to have their students and teachers watch the president's speech "so they can compete in the global economy." Duncan told them to make use of the "Menu of classroom activities for grades PreK–6 and for grades 7–12."

The PreK–6 Menu tells teachers to "build background knowledge about the President" by reading books about Barack Obama. The Menu tells elementary students it is "important that we listen to the President," to "take notes while President Obama is talking," to "write down key ideas or phrases" from his speech, and to "discuss them after the speech." The Menu instructs teachers to "extend learning" of PreK–6 children by having them "write letters to themselves about how they can achieve their short-term and long-term education goals." Their letters are to be "collected and redistributed at an appropriate later date by the teacher to make students accountable to their goals."

The Menu for grades 7–12 instructs teachers to post "notable quotes" from Obama's speeches on the board, and to have students "take notes while President Obama talks" and identify "the three most important words in the speech." Students should be queried: "What is President Obama inspiring you to do?" and "How will he inspire us?"

The hero worship and brainwashing built into these lesson plans are, to say the least, inappropriate. Parents should rise up and stop the public schools from using classroom or assembly time to teach schoolchildren to be cheerleaders for Obama and his policies.

Now comes the iron fist in the velvet glove. President Obama's nearly trillion-dollar Stimulus law designated $128 billion for education, so it's no surprise that tight strings were attached.

Buried in the fine print is an ominous requirement to build a national electronic database of all children. Any state that receives federal education funds must "establish a longitudinal data system that includes the elements described in ... the America COMPETES Act."

That law, passed in 2007, sets out the goal of longitudinal databasing of "student-level enrollment, demographic, and program participation information" for all students from preschool through postsecondary education. This electronic database will contain "yearly test records of individual students," "a teacher identifier system with the ability to match teachers to students," "student-level transcript information, including information on courses completed and grades earned," and "student-level college readiness test scores."

Database collection on each student continues through college and into the workforce. States are required to enter "information regarding the extent to which students transition successfully from secondary school to postsecondary education."

Creation of a database of this magnitude is the sort of thing that totalitarian governments do, but it should not be allowed by those who value freedom. It's appalling to think of Obama's czars and political operatives having access to all that personal information on American citizens. But this is part and parcel of Obama's hope and change.

He is indeed the one the left has "been waiting for." *San Francisco Chronicle* online columnist Mark Morford predicted that Obama was not just going to transform America or the world but also mankind's relation to the whole planet.

In 2008, Morford wrote that he had been told by "spiritually advanced people I know (not coweringly religious, mind you, but deeply spiritual)" that Obama was a "Lightworker, that rare kind of attuned being who has the ability to lead us not merely to new foreign policies or health care plans or whatnot, but who can actually help usher in *a new way of being on the planet*, of relating and connecting and engaging with this bizarre earthly experiment."

This cult of Obama continues in the campaign rhetoric of 2012—a cult Obama carefully cultivates through his rhetoric of revolution, seeing himself not so much as a president, but as a supreme revolutionary leader or head of a church.

In 2009, his former communications director Anita Dunn told students at a Washington-area high school that her "favorite political philosopher" was Chairman Mao, the Marxist leader who killed millions in twentieth-century China and crushed Christian churches. Dunn left the White House tarnished by this remark, but her admiration for revolutionary power is widely held there, including by the president himself. When Obama finally decided on his 2012 campaign slogan, he chose a word with eerie Maoist echoes—"Forward." Will Americans join him? Will the cult of Obama triumph? Or will Americans at long last reassert their God-given freedoms? The stakes are high, and the choice is ours.

APPENDIX ONE

Cardinal Dolan's letter to his fellow bishops, reiterating the
Church's resolve to resist Obama's assault on religious freedom

Office of the President

3211 FOURTH STREET NE · WASHINGTON DC 20017-1194 · 202-541-3100 · FAX 202-541-3166

Cardinal Timothy M. Dolan
Archbishop of New York
President

March 2, 2012

My brother bishops,

Twice in recent weeks, I have written you to express my gratitude for our unity in faith and action as we move forward to protect our *religious freedom* from unprecedented intrusion from a government bureau, the Department of Health and Human Services (HHS). I remain deeply grateful to you for your determined resolve, to the Chairmen of our committees directly engaged in these efforts - Cardinal Daniel DiNardo, Cardinal Donald Wuerl, Bishop Stephen Blaire and Bishop William Lori -who have again shown themselves to be such excellent leaders during these past weeks, and to all our staff at the USCCB who work so diligently under the direction of the Conference leadership.

How fortunate that we as a body have had opportunities during our past plenary assemblies to manifest our strong unity in defense of *religious freedom*. We rely on that unity now more than ever as HHS seeks to define what constitutes church ministry and how it can be exercised. We will once again dedicate ample time at our Administrative Committee meeting next week, and at the June Plenary Assembly, to this critical subject. We will continue to listen, discuss, deliberate and act.

Thank you, brothers, for the opportunity to provide this update to you and the dioceses you serve.   Many of you have expressed your thanks for what we have achieved together in so few weeks, especially the data provided and the leadership given by brother bishops, our conference staff and Catholic faithful. And you now ask the obvious question, "What's next?" Please allow me to share with you now some thoughts about events and efforts to date and where we might go next.

Since January 20, when the final, restrictive HHS Rule was first announced, we have become certain of two things: *religious freedom* is under attack, and we will not cease our struggle to protect it. We recall the words of our Holy Father Benedict XVI to our brother bishops on their recent *ad limina* visit: "Of particular concern are certain attempts being made to limit that most cherished of American freedoms, the freedom of religion." Bishop Stephen Blaire and Bishop William Lori, with so many others, have admirably kept us focused on this one priority of protecting *religious freedom*. We have made it clear in no uncertain terms to the government that we are not at peace with its invasive attempt to curtail the *religious freedom* we cherish as Catholics and Americans. We did not ask for this fight, but we will not run from it.

As pastors and shepherds, each of us would prefer to spend our energy engaged in and promoting the works of mercy to which the Church is dedicated: healing the sick, teaching our youth, and helping the poor. Yet, precisely because we are pastors and shepherds, we recognize that each of the ministries entrusted to us by Jesus is now in jeopardy due to this bureaucratic intrusion into the internal life of the church. You and I both know well that we were doing those extensive and noble works rather well without these radical new constrictive and forbidding mandates. Our Church has a long tradition of effective partnership with government and the wider community in the service of the sick, our children, our elders, and the poor at home and abroad, and we sure hope to continue it.

Of course, we maintained from the start that this is not a "Catholic" fight alone. I like to quote as often as possible a nurse who emailed me, "I'm not so much mad about all this as a Catholic, but as an American." And as we recall, a Baptist minister, Governor Mike Huckabee, observed, "In this matter, we're all Catholics." No doubt you have heard numerous statements just like these. We are grateful to know so many of our fellow Americans, especially our friends in the ecumenical and interreligious dialogue, stand together in this important moment in our country. They know that this is not just about sterilization, abortifacients, and chemical contraception. It's about *religious freedom*, the sacred right of any Church to define its own teaching and ministry.

When the President announced on January 20th that the choking mandates from HHS would remain, not only we bishops and our Catholic faithful, but people of every faith, or none at all, rallied in protest. The worry that we had expressed -- that such government control was contrary to our deepest political values -- was eloquently articulated by constitutional scholars and leaders of every creed.

On February 10th, the President announced that the insurance providers would have to pay the bill, instead of the Church's schools, hospitals, clinics, or vast network of charitable outreach having to do so. He considered this "concession" adequate. Did this help? We wondered if it would, and you will recall that the Conference announced at first that, while withholding final judgment, we would certainly give the President's proposal close scrutiny. Well, we did -- and as you know, we are as worried as ever.

For one, there was not even a nod to the deeper concerns about trespassing upon *religious freedom*, or of modifying the HHS' attempt to define the how and who of our ministry. Two, since a big part of our ministries are "self-insured," we still ask how this protects us. We'll still have to pay and, in addition to that, we'll still have to maintain in our policies practices which our Church has consistently taught are grave wrongs in which we cannot participate. And what about forcing individual believers to pay for what violates their *religious freedom* and conscience? We can't abandon the hard working person of faith who has a right to *religious freedom*. And three, there was still no resolution about the handcuffs placed upon renowned Catholic charitable agencies, both national and international, and their exclusion from contracts just because they will not refer victims of human trafficking, immigrants and refugees, and the hungry of the world, for abortions, sterilization, or contraception. In many ways, the announcement of February 10 solved little and complicated a lot. We now have more questions than answers, more confusion than clarity.

So the important question arises: What to do now? How can we bishops best respond, especially united in our common pastoral ministry as an Episcopal Conference? For one, under the ongoing leadership of Cardinal Daniel DiNardo, Cardinal Donald Wuerl, Bishop Blaire and Bishop Lori we will continue our strong efforts of advocacy and education. In the coming weeks the Conference will continue to provide you, among other things, with catechetical resources on the significance of *religious freedom* to the Church and the Church's teaching on it from a doctrinal and moral perspective. We are developing liturgical aids to encourage prayer in our efforts and plans on how we can continue to voice our public and strong opposition to this infringement on our freedom. And the Ad Hoc Committee on Religious Liberty, that has served

2

the Conference so well in its short lifespan, will continue its extraordinary work in service to this important cause.

Two, we will ardently continue to seek a rescinding of the suffocating mandates that require us to violate our moral convictions, or at least insist upon a much wider latitude to the exemptions so that churches can be free of the new, rigidly narrow definition of church, minister and ministry that would prevent us from helping those in need, educating children and healing the sick, no matter their religion.

In this regard, the President invited us to "work out the wrinkles." We have accepted that invitation. Unfortunately, this seems to be stalled: the White House Press Secretary, for instance, informed the nation that the mandates are a *fait accompli* (and, embarrassingly for him, commented that we bishops have always opposed Health Care anyway, a charge that is scurrilous and insulting, not to mention flat out wrong. Bishop Blaire did a fine job of setting the record straight.) The White House already notified Congress that the dreaded mandates are now published in the Federal Registry "without change." The Secretary of HHS is widely quoted as saying, "Religious insurance companies don't really design the plans they sell based on their own religious tenets." That doesn't bode well for their getting a truly acceptable "accommodation."

At a recent meeting between staff of the bishops' conference and the White House staff, our staff members asked directly whether the broader concerns of *religious freedom*—that is, revisiting the straight-jacketing mandates, or broadening the maligned exemption—are all off the table. They were informed that they are. So much for "working out the wrinkles." Instead, they advised the bishops' conference that we should listen to the "enlightened" voices of accommodation, such as the recent, hardly surprising yet terribly unfortunate editorial in *America*. The White House seems to think we bishops simply do not know or understand Catholic teaching and so, taking a cue from its own definition of *religious freedom*, now has nominated its own handpicked official Catholic teachers.

We will continue to accept invitations to meet with and to voice our concerns to anyone of any party, for this is hardly partisan, who is willing to correct the infringements on *religious freedom* that we are now under. But as we do so, we cannot rely on off the record promises of fixes without deadlines and without assurances of proposals that will concretely address the concerns in a manner that does not conflict with our principles and teaching.

Congress might provide more hope, since thoughtful elected officials have proposed legislation to protect what should be so obvious: *religious freedom*. Meanwhile, in our recent debate in the senate, our opponents sought to obscure what is really a *religious freedom* issue by maintaining that abortion inducing drugs and the like are a "woman's health issue." We will not let this deception stand. Our commitment to seeking legislative remedies remains strong. And it is about remedies to the assault on *religious freedom*. Period. (By the way, the Church hardly needs to be lectured about health care for women. Thanks mostly to our Sisters, the Church is the largest private provider of health care for women and their babies in the country.) Bishop William Lori, Chairman of our *Ad Hoc Committee on Religious Liberty*, stated it well in a recent press release: "We will build on this base of support as we pursue legislation in the House of Representatives, urge the Administration to change its course on this issue, and explore our legal rights under the Constitution and the Religious Freedom Restoration Act."

Perhaps the courts offer the most light. In the recent *Hosanna-Tabor* ruling, the Supreme Court unanimously defended the right of a Church to define its own ministry and services, a dramatic rebuff to the administration, apparently unheeded by the White House. Thus, our bishops' conference, many individual religious entities, and other people of good will are working with some top-notch law firms who feel so strongly about this that they will represent us *pro-bono*. In the upcoming days, you will hear much more about this encouraging and welcome development.

Given this climate, we have to prepare for tough times. Some, like *America* magazine, want us to cave-in and stop fighting, saying this is simply a policy issue; some want us to close everything down rather than comply (In an excellent article, Cardinal Francis George wrote that the administration apparently wants us to "give up for Lent" our schools, hospitals, and charitable ministries); some, like Bishop Robert Lynch wisely noted, wonder whether we might have to engage in civil disobedience and risk steep fines; some worry that we'll have to face a decision between two ethically repugnant choices: subsidizing immoral services or no longer offering insurance coverage, a road none of us wants to travel.

Brothers, we know so very well that *religious freedom* is our heritage, our legacy and our firm belief, both as loyal Catholics and Americans. There have been many threats to *religious freedom* over the decades and years, but these often came from without. This one sadly comes from within. As our ancestors did with previous threats, we will tirelessly defend the timeless and enduring truth of *religious freedom*.

I look forward to our upcoming Administrative Board Meeting and our June Plenary Assembly when we will have the chance to discuss together these important issues and our way forward in addressing them. And I renew my thanks to you for your tremendous, fraternal support and your welcome observations in this critical effort to protect our *religious freedom*.

With prayerful best wishes, I am

Fraternally in Christ,

Timothy Cardinal Dolan
Archbishop of New York
President, United States Conference of Catholic Bishops

APPENDIX TWO

**Calumet
Community
Religious
Conference**

COPY
of an original document hou
ARCHIVES OF Th
ARCHDIOCESE OF CH
This is a red ink stamp!
DO NOT COPY

20 May 1986

Dear Sharon:

Enclosed is a requisition order for the ticket purchased for my
trip to the IAF Training in Los Angeles, as well as a xerox
copy of the ticket itself. Hope this is sufficient for reimbursement. Call me or Jerry if we need to exchange more information
regarding IAF Training or the workshop in August.

Regards,

Barack Obama

553 Hirsch Avenue, Calumet City, Illinois 60409   351 East 113th Street, Chicago, Illinois 60628
(312) 995-8189

Barack Obama's letter to the archdiocese of Chicago, asking it to reimburse him
for his plane fare to an "IAF training" conference in Los Angeles in 1986. IAF
stands for the Industrial Areas Foundation, the radical group founded by Saul
Alinsky. The documents in this and the following appendix confirm the unholy
alliance between Obama and the archdiocese of Chicago under Cardinal Joseph
Bernardin in their joint pursuit of socialist organizing.

Campaign for Human Development

155 EAST SUPERIOR STREET • CHICAGO, ILLINOIS 60611 • (312) 751 - 8390

M E M O R A N D U M

To: Barack Obama

From: Sharon Jacobson _SJ_

Date: June 30, 1986

Re: Reimbursement for the IAF Training Trip

Enclosed please find a check in the amount of $196.00. This represents the cost of the trip to California for the IAF training.

I'm glad that both you and John Owens plan to attend the training. I'm anxious to hear of your impressions of this experience. Have a good trip.

THE CATHOLIC BISHOP OF CHICAGO
P. O. BOX 1979
CHICAGO, ILLINOIS 60690

THE FIRST NATIONAL BANK
OF CHICAGO
CHICAGO, ILLINOIS

No. 047441

2-1
710

	CHECK NO.	DATE	AMOUNT
PAY $196.00	047441	6/20/86	**$****196.00

TO THE
ORDER OF   CALUMET COMMUNITY RELIGIOUS
CONFERENCE

THE CATHOLIC BISHOP OF CHICAGO

A 15

⑈000474411⑈ ⑈071000013⑈ 50 24439⑈

*"Action on behalf of justice and participation in the transformation of the world fully appear to us as a constitutive dimension of the preaching of the Gospel, or, in other words, of the Church's mission for the redemption of the human race and its liberation from every oppressive situation."
— 1971 World Synod of Catholic Bishops

The check to Obama from the archdiocese of Chicago for his plane fare to an Alinskyite "IAF training" conference. This is graphic evidence that the Church in America bred her own destroyer. Notice also the jargony, euphemism-laden socialist tribute to "transformation" from a 1971 world synod of bishops below the check.

Obama's invoice to the archdiocese of Chicago. The "Campaign for Human Development" to which the invoice refers was the archdiocese's Alinskyite "social justice" office.

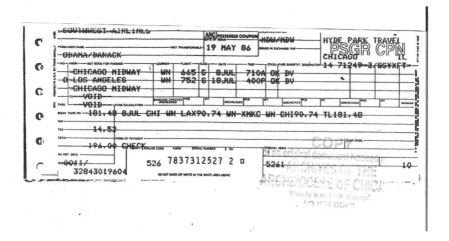

The copy of Obama's plane ticket to Los Angeles for "IAF training."

APPENDIX THREE

Chicago Homecare Organizing Project
33 East Congress
Chicago, IL 60605

20,000

Contact: Keith Kelleher
         # 939 - 7490

IOPGC Near West Project
Interfaith Organizing Project of Greater Chicago
1613 W. Washington
Chicago, IL 60612

$30,000

Contact: Ed Shurna
         # 243 - 3328

The Developing Communities Project
Calumet Community Religious Conference
351 E. 113th Street
Chicago, IL 60628

33,000

Contact: Barack Obama
         # 995 - 8182

Homesteaders Rights Project
Chicago ACORN
33 E. Congress, 1-B
Chicago, IL 60605

$30,000

Contact: Madeline Talbott
         # 939 -7488

ACE Community Organizing
Action Coalition of Englewood
6220 S. Sangamon
Chicago, IL 60621

20,000

Contact: Mindy Linetsky
         # 471 - 0080

Low Income Cooperative Work & Ownership in
   New Housing Technology
Bethel New Life, Inc.
367 N. Karlov
Chicago, IL 60624

30,000

Contact: Mary Nelson
         # 826 5540

Financial Industry Partnership Project
National Training and Information Center
954 W. Washington
Chicago, IL 60607

$20,000

Contact: Shel Trapp
         # 243 - 3035

Proof that the Catholic Campaign for Human Development gave a $33,000 grant to Obama for his socialist organizing.

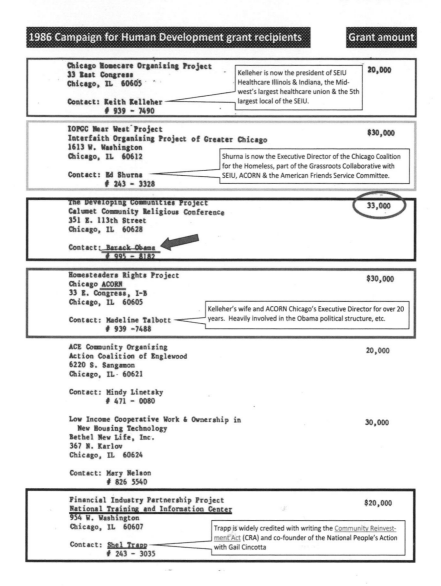

1986 Campaign for Human Development grant recipients	Grant amount

Chicago Homecare Organizing Project
33 East Congress
Chicago, IL 60605

Contact: Keith Kelleher
939 - 7490

20,000

Kelleher is now the president of SEIU Healthcare Illinois & Indiana, the Midwest's largest healthcare union & the 5th largest local of the SEIU.

IOPGC Near West Project
Interfaith Organizing Project of Greater Chicago
1613 W. Washington
Chicago, IL 60612

Contact: Ed Shurna
243 - 3328

$30,000

Shurna is now the Executive Director of the Chicago Coalition for the Homeless, part of the Grassroots Collaborative with SEIU, ACORN & the American Friends Service Committee.

The Developing Communities Project
Calumet Community Religious Conference
351 E. 113th Street
Chicago, IL 60628

Contact: Barack Obama
995 - 8182

33,000

Homesteaders Rights Project
Chicago ACORN
33 E. Congress, I-B
Chicago, IL 60605

Contact: Madeline Talbott
939 -7488

$30,000

Kelleher's wife and ACORN Chicago's Executive Director for over 20 years. Heavily involved in the Obama political structure, etc.

ACE Community Organizing
Action Coalition of Englewood
6220 S. Sangamon
Chicago, IL 60621

Contact: Mindy Linetsky
471 - 0080

20,000

Low Income Cooperative Work & Ownership in
New Housing Technology
Bethel New Life, Inc.
367 N. Karlov
Chicago, IL 60624

Contact: Mary Nelson
826 5540

30,000

Financial Industry Partnership Project
National Training and Information Center
954 W. Washington
Chicago, IL 60607

Contact: Shel Trapp
243 - 3035

$20,000

Trapp is widely credited with writing the Community Reinvestment Act (CRA) and co-founder of the National People's Action with Gail Cincotta

A list of some of the Catholic Campaign for Human Development's grant recipients, including Obama and other pivotal figures in socialist organizing.

APPENDIX FOUR

A draft of a letter from Bishop Norbert Gaughan pressuring priests in the dioceses of Chicago and Gary to cooperate with Obama (the "Gerald Kellman" to whom Gaughan refers was Obama's direct boss) in his socialist organizing

DRAFT OF LETTER FROM BISHOP GAUGHAN TO PASTORS

Dear Father,

Cardinal Bernardin has written to me to suggest that the Archdiocese of Chicago and the Diocese of Gary work together on the severe social and economic problems of the Bi-State area. After meeting with Bishop Wilton Gregory, Episcopal Vicar of Vicariate VI in Chicago, I have asked Gerald Kellman, who works with Vicariate VI to contact you. Vicariate VI includes the Southeast side of the City of Chicago and South Suburban Cook County. It is the Illinois portion of our Calumet Region. Mr. Kellman directs a program which addresses these problems for the Archdiocese.

He will ask to make an appointment with you to listen to

(1) how these community and economic concerns are affecting your parish.

(2) your ideas on an appropriate pastoral response for your parish and the Diocese.

(3) which lay persons can work with the parish and the Diocese in developing a coordinated grass-roots strategy to address these concerns.

I am sure you share my concern for our people, who are affected by these problems. As our National Conference of Bishops completes the final draft of our pastoral letter on the economy, it is appropriate that we search for ways to implement the gospel message which inspires our pastoral through concrete action. I will be working closely with Mr. Kellman on this effort. Please give him your support and cooperation.

ACKNOWLEDGMENTS

The authors would like to thank Harry Crocker, Regnery's vice president and executive editor, for conceiving this project and for his sharp editing and direction. The authors also thank Regnery's senior editor Thomas Spence for his kind intervention and Regnery's managing editor Mary Beth Baker for her copyediting.

George Neumayr: I thank Mel Berger, my agent at William Morris Endeavor, for representing me through the twists and turns of this book project. The following people also provided research help or commiseration during the project, for which I am grateful: Kimberly Guilfoyle, John Zmirak, Rey Flores, Jeremy Lott, Thomas McArdle, Roger McCaffrey, Thomas Pauken, Elaine Donnelly, Brooks Braden, Daniel Allott, and Michele Diatta.

Thanks also to my siblings (Mary, John, Catherine, Thomas, Jane, and Anne), and to my parents (John and Bridget), through whom I received the Roman Catholic faith. My zeal for the book's theme derives from Jesus Christ's teaching that the fulfillment of human nature is union with the triune God—an eternal friendship, beginning in this life and culminating in the next one, that no government has the right to corrupt or impede.

INDEX